Smaller Citizens

Smaller Citizens

Writings on the Making of Indian Citizens

Krishna Kumar

Orient BlackSwan

SMALLER CITIZENS

ORIENT BLACKSWAN PRIVATE LIMITED

Registered Office
3-6-752 Himayatnagar, Hyderabad 500 029, Telangana, India
Email: centraloffice@orientblackswan.com

Other Offices
Bengaluru, Chennai, Guwahati, Hyderabad, Kolkata,
Mumbai, New Delhi, Noida, Patna

First published 2021
Reprinted 2022

040443

ISBN 978-93-5442-080-1

Typeset in Crimson 11/13 *by*
Shine Graphics, Delhi 110 094

Printed at
Avantika Printers Private Limited, New Delhi 110 020

Published by
Orient Blackswan Private Limited
3-6-752, Himayatnagar, Hyderabad 500 029, Telangana, India
Email: info@orientblackswan.com

For Latika and her students

Contents

Publisher's Acknowledgements

'Studying Childhood.' First published as 'Studying Childhood in India' in the *Economic and Political Weekly*, vol. 51, issue no. 23, 4 June 2016.

'Education and Girlhood.' First published in the *Economic and Political Weekly*, vol. 52, issue no. 47, 25 November 2017.

'Rurality, Modernity and Education.' First published in the *Economic and Political Weekly*, vol. 49, issue no. 22, 31 May 2014.

Quoted material from 'Let a Hundred Children Blossom', *The Hindu*, 20 April 2012. Reproduced with permission of The Hindu Group.

'Equality under a Post-Welfare State.' Originally published as 'Universal Schooling and Equality: Right to Education under a Post-Welfare State', MIDS working paper no. 228, June 2018. Reproduced with permission of the Madras Institute of Development Studies (MIDS).

'Education and Poverty.' Originally published as 'Where Knowledge is Poor', *The Hindu*, 12 October 2013. Reproduced with permission of the Hindu Group.

'The Death of a Small Boy.' First published in *The Hindu*, 18 December 2012. Reproduced with permission of the Hindu Group.

'Leela Dube's Poser.' Originally published as 'A Messy Corner of India's Modernity', *The Hindu*, 30 June 2012. Reproduced with permission of the Hindu Group.

'Education and Caste.' Originally published as 'The Curriculum Taboo', by Krishna Kumar, first published in *The Indian Express*, 7 July 2018. Reprinted with permission of The Indian Express (P) Limited © 2018. All rights reserved.

'Peasants as Citizens.' Originally published as 'Written-off in the Hinterland', *The Hindu*, 3 July 2017. Reproduced with permission of the Hindu Group.

'The Essentialised Village.' Originally published as 'Let us not Essentialize the Village', *The Hindu*, 27 May 2015. Reproduced with permission of the Hindu Group.

'Adolescent Voices.' Originally published as 'Listen to These Four Girls: On the Panapakkam Suicides', *The Hindu*, 29 December 2017. Reproduced with permission of the Hindu Group.

'Remembering a Baiga Woman.' Originally published as 'Chaiti Bai's Story and Modern India', *The Hindu,* 29 November 2014. Reproduced with permission of the Hindu Group.

'The Temptation to Take a Picture.' Originally published as 'The Temptation to Go Viral', *The Hindu,* 10 February 2017. Reproduced with permission of the Hindu Group.

'A Matter of Belief.' Originally published in *Seminar,* issue no. 369, November 1989. Reproduced with permission of *Seminar.*

'Citizens and the Bureaucracy.' Originally published as 'The Lone Voice of Pankajakshi Amma', *The Hindu,* 5 May 2016. Reproduced with permission of the Hindu Group.

'A Pedagogy of Freedom and Peace.' Originally published as 'A Theory for Education and Peace' in *The Making of a Modern Indian Artist-Craftsman: Devi Prasad,* edited by Naman P. Ahuja, pp. 123–29, Routledge India, 2011. Reproduced with permission of the Licensor through PLSclear.

Prologue

As the Shatabdi Express draws close to its destination, a voice on the public address system asks the passengers to destroy the mineral water bottles given to them at the start of the journey. They are given the alternative of taking the bottles with them. Both steps, the official announcement clarifies, will 'avoid misuse'. A few passengers take their half-empty bottles with them. Most of them choose the first option and destroy the bottles. Their collective crunching creates a loud sound that sweeps along the compartment for a few seconds. It conveys how successful education has been in nurturing a compliant middle-class citizenry wherein those who worry about the environmental risk posed by a crunched-up plastic bottle constitute a tiny minority. For the rest, instant compliance with the state's advice is perhaps the best evidence of being well educated. The impulse to comply has been ingrained into reliable daily habits by hard-working teachers and principals of effective schools. They have left little room in the citizen's mind for imagining where the crumpled plastic bottle will go next. They simply drop it on the floor after crushing it. Someone will have to collect these shapeless pieces of clear plastic. The thought that every crushed bottle will end up on a little hillock of garbage on the outskirts of the city does not invade the privileged citizen's mind. That the garbage will ultimately catch fire and the crushed plastic bottle will smoulder for a long time, making its own little addition to the poisoned city air, is even more alien to the decently educated mind.

The middle-class mind tends to ignore the hard life of the functionaries who carry out the logistics of the surrounding world. The sweepers who will collect the garbage from the railway compartments, the toilet cleaners, the garbage collectors and the garbage sorters belong to a world rather far removed from the one to which the privileged passengers of the Shatabdi Express belong.

The latter constitute an important segment of the urban middle class. They may occasionally feel angry with the state, but they generally identify with it. Instant compliance with the state's order or advice sits nicely with the conventional ideal of an educated citizen. Many of the Shatabdi passengers have in all probability attended schools affiliated to the Central Board of Secondary Education (CBSE), where some of the teachers might have tried to teach them how to question or think critically and imaginatively. However, this part of their learning at school neither helped them fetch them good marks in the Board exam, nor did it suffice to counter the effects of hard routines that create and consolidate reliable habits of compliance with orders from above.

This everyday incident helps us to recognise a paradox that lies at the heart of modern education. It is expected to make children capable of thinking for themselves, yet the process makes them thoughtlessly compliant. The paradox refers to the simultaneity of the intellectual and civic functions of mass schooling. The former aims at nurturing freedom of the individual, the latter at grooming the regimented citizen. Modern societies have assigned to schools the responsibility to promote these contradictory capacities in the common citizen at a young age. As a social institution, the school fulfils these expectations, and in the process, creates or exacerbates a tension that society must endure, both within itself and in its relationship with the state.

This duality and tension in the political potential of education is highly relevant for any attempt to make sense of Indian democracy. Governed by a socially progressive Constitution, the state in India functions with norms and structures established under colonial rule. The Constitution provides overarching guidance for the state to follow, in terms of values and goals, but the state's history and accumulated experience carries its guiding power. The various components and structures of the state's apparatus function under norms and procedures that don't necessarily find adequate guidance, either critical or positive, from the pithy discourse of the Constitution. The system of education is one such structure. How efficiently does this particular structure serve the socially transformative agenda of the Constitution? The essays and lectures included in this book engage with this question.

The reader might find this engagement to be mostly critical. This is a reflection of the distance that separates the constitutional ideals from the everyday functioning of the apparatus available to the state for dealing with education. Questions may arise in the reader's mind about reforms envisaged all along since Independence. Questions like 'What happened to these reforms?' or 'Why didn't these reforms make a greater impact?' are certainly worth exploring, and some of the lectures included in the first part of the book do precisely that.

The writings included in this book attempt to examine and engage with this tension between the intellectual and the civic functions of schooling. There are two reasons why this examination may interest the reader. One is that it may provide some help in understanding the complexities of education, as an idea and as a system. The other reason is that it may offer readers, especially those involved in the system of education, direction in terms of ways to mitigate the tension. The tension I am referring to expresses itself rather strongly along the axis of inequality, causing conflict or sharpening an existing conflict. Different dimensions of inequality that are relevant to education have been actively noted and investigated over the recent decades. The gap between the richer and the poorer strata is so widely recognised that it now arouses little interest. An equilibrium has emerged between the egalitarian mandate of the state and the social ethos—also promoted by the state—that has moved towards market solutions based on private provision. Inequalities are increasing, and attempts to bridge the gap between the privileged and the underprivileged evoke resentment among the former. One instance is the response to the reservation provided in the Right to Education (RTE) Act for one-fourth of private school seats for economically weaker children. This provision continues to be criticised and resisted by private schools. Caste-based reservation, although much older and more entrenched in the system, also continues to stoke anger among the upper castes.

The urban–rural gap is another familiar axis of educational inequality. Awareness of this form of inequality has diminished, rather than grown, with time. The assumption that urbanisation signifies development constitutes a wide overlap between scholarly and policy circles. It underpins the 'hope' that the 'rural population' will shrink as a result of destitution and migration, and the vast multitudes of migrants will gain better access to services in urban slums. This perspective enables the state to maintain a low-energy interest in the life lived in villages. This is reflected in the neglect of rural schools. It is scaffolded by the belief that the smarter among rural children, who survive in the education system, will seek their destiny in cities. This pattern was entrenched in the system of education during the colonial period, and it continues to underpin the policy scenario. The state has failed to develop any imagination that might be applicable specifically to the rural child.

Gender forms another dimension of inequality discussed in some of the writings in this volume. Compared to class inequality and the urban–rural disparity, the gender gap has received more active attention in recent years. The gap has been measured mostly in terms of enrolment and retention. These are, of course, important elements of the study of inequality between boys and girls, but the difference in their educational experience is a more serious matter. My interest in this area has forced me to look at the history of both policy and culture, or rather, the history of the state's reluctance to deal with culture. That history has not ended though India is no longer under colonial rule and is free to engage critically with its cultural problems. Apparently, the risk involved in engaging with the tension underlying gender inequality is perceived to be great, and the resources available are measly.

My attempt to respond to India's educational problems has always impelled me to look back. It offers a perspective to make sense of the present, but it also helps me to endure the anguish I experience when I learn about the difficulties children face in their lives and at the schools they attend. In this volume, there are a few essays that look at the past. Hopefully, they will arouse the reader's interest in history, and also extend the help that historical understanding can provide for engaging with present-day realities. Ultimately, any enquiry into education expresses a desire to find space for peaceful movement into the future. Long-standing contradictions and unaddressed problems make the immediate future of education look unusually tough. Had I been trained in the modern science of management, I might have preferred the term 'challenge' over the older term, 'problem'. But a problem becomes a challenge only if someone accepts it. Neither society nor state seem to have accepted education as an area of challenges. Exciting though they are, they have been begging for recognition, of their substance and scale, for a long time.

Equality, justice and fraternity are treated as the basic values of the Constitution. Although the Constitution, in its original form, did not include education as a fundamental right, it now includes it in the category of such rights. However, only the elementary stage is covered, and that too for the specific age-group of six to fourteen. Even this limited coverage looks like a bold step, given the social context wherein a generous sanction exists for indifference to childhood as a formative stage of life. Indeed, the idea of childhood is applicable in Indian society in a rather limited sense. It remains essentially a biological concept. As a social category, childhood is yet to gain acceptance in the context of girls and vast sections of the labouring poor. We can say that childhood is a major site of struggle for structural change in the social order. In many respects, the struggle is quite bitter and causes a great amount of persistent stress. Education witnesses this stress and adds to it. As a social institution, education is supposed to make economic and cultural conflicts bearable, and it does play this role in India. At the same time, it also serves as a source of conflict. This is why its study and reform call for reflection on peace. Anyone who wishes to engage with education as a system, with the intention of improving it in any sense, must be prepared to deal with conflicts. They will arise in the course of any action, modest or major, both in the functional sphere of institutional life and in the curricular sphere where ideas and images contend for space and treatment. A peaceful resolution is necessary for all such conflicts if education is to make progress rather than stagnate and become an instrument of conservation alone. However, peace is not merely a matter of resolving conflicts; it also constitutes a search for balance and justified accommodation. In the terribly unjust social order that we live in, peace implies the pursuit of justice through education. And that does not mean teaching or preaching justice. It has to be experienced by children in their everyday life at school, at the hands of a teacher who is aware of the scale and types of injustice that any child can sense in the air, irrespective of the social location. Schools and colleges socialise the young to ignore the world or fear it, rather than approach it with the passion to understand it and engage with it. That is the job that the system of education is not performing at present.

If peace is to be regarded as a major concern for education, the history teachers and curriculum designers must be viewed as carrying a special responsibility. Although all aspects of social learning require the young to understand how things came to be as they are now, the specific teacher of history is centrally involved in creating attitudes towards the past and towards its influence on the present. I have been particularly concerned in this respect with the role that the teaching of modern history has played in socialising the young in India and Pakistan into a ritualised acceptance of a politically charged relationship between the two countries. It is not merely how Partition is treated in the curriculum and textbooks, but also the manner in which regimentation of nationalist ideas and feelings occurs in both countries through texts, school rituals and the media. This vast theme occupies two of my earlier books, *Prejudice and Pride* (2001), and *Battle for Peace* (2007). In this volume, I have included some of my recent, shorter writings on the subject, along with a lecture-essay on the question: 'Can education contribute to peace?' The answer to this question cannot be simple because it involves not merely a change in the history curriculum but also a broader reform in the system of education. Like most other key questions raised in this volume, this one too requires a better understanding of the problem rather than an immediate solution. This is because the latter cannot have much meaning if the system of education is unable to spread or sustain the solution for a length of time required by any educational effort to make a difference.

1

Studying Childhood

This lecture was the keynote address delivered at the seminar on 'Contested Sites: Construction of Childhood', held at the Indian Institute of Advanced Study in Shimla, between 26 and 28 November 2015.

Our ability to use 'childhood' as an analytical term depends on the amount and type of knowledge we possess about parenting, teaching, children's literature and children themselves—both past and present. These are distinct areas of scholarly endeavour, and none of them is particularly well developed in our academic institutions. So, as we gather here to discuss childhood, we must recognise the limitations set upon our aims by the availability of knowledge. A major dimension of the limitations relates to the diversity of circumstances in which childhood unfolds in our country. 'Diversity' is a deceptive term; it highlights attractive differences arising from geography and culture, while seeking to keep out of view the differences arising from inequality rooted in economic conditions and the caste hierarchy. When applied to childhood, diversity also tends to place under a cover the sharp differentiation induced by culture over gender. It may not be all that untrue to say that when it comes to poverty and the female gender, childhood in India is not particularly diverse. We will also have to recognise 'rural' and 'urban' as categories relevant to the study of childhood. Their relevance is, in fact, growing as India's modernity passes through increasingly impatient phases of economic development. Indeed, we may have to recognise new categories such as 'childhood under forced displacement' just as the UN has recognised 'childhood in difficult circumstances' arising from war and endemic violence.

Our contemplation of childhood in India is likely to be framed by the dominant global discourse on the subject. Its normative character has its uses, but it also enforces an essentialised vision and a compulsively comparative outlook on our attempts to study the childhood that surrounds us. The problem is linked to the training our curiosity has received under a colonised system of education. We tend to look either for a replication of the European experience or we yearn for reactive contrast. Colonialism as the mother-ideology of the modern world leaves its academic progeny with limited options. Moreover, our discourse is shaped by the location of our intended audience. Any new project of knowledge must keep these constraints in mind, and this applies rather more to research-starved areas like childhood.

The child, as a discourse of freedom, individuality and equality, was born in mid-eighteenth century in Western Europe. This constellation of terms lies at the heart of pedagogic modernism and the practice of setting childhood sharply apart from adulthood—a practice which had already been in the making for 150 years when, among others, Montessori and then Piaget etched the contours of childhood. Both did it by locating the growth of the young mind in biology. But a major shift had already occurred in the study of life in relation to its environment. Studies of childhood inspired by the theory of behaviourism look simplistic, and are rightly criticised today, but it attained a major victory over theories of inherited capacities by highlighting the role of the environment. In a parallel development, Freudian psychoanalysis demonstrated the formative nature of early childhood experience. The somewhat deterministic explanation offered by Freud drove social and political processes to make children's education and health the highest priority. Scholarship in different academic areas questioned the deterministic element in Freud's theory, leading to advancements in a range of early childhood care practices. Western debates between different schools of theorisation about learning proceeded in early twentieth century in a politically dynamic ethos shaped by democratic struggles of different kinds. In the course of its own political development, Europe found many different answers to Rousseau's questioning of the idea of the loyal citizen. Rousseau's engagement was centred in the child endowed by nature with freedom. How would such a child be educated? This key question underlies the history of educational progress and contradictions between child-centric pedagogy and education for citizenship.

More often than not, we fail to recognise and appreciate these matters. Nor do we attempt to interpret their implications for our colonial context. And this is not because we lack guidance. We have had excellent teachers on this matter—teachers of the stature of Gandhi and Tagore. Carrying forward their legacy, Devi Prasad heard the child as a culture in distress, craving for the means to express itself when its life had been squeezed out of its body. As duly colonised citizens of India, we have been too busy in national development to listen to these teachers with attention. We do need to study our political history more imaginatively. If we agree to do so, we will notice a transformative moment when the child became a trope of independent nationhood. This semiotic event occurred in the 1930s, after Gandhi established himself as a magician leader who could turn common salt into collective passion. 'Idgaah', a short story by Premchand, captures this moment. Its hero, a poor Muslim child, browbeats his richer neighbours by his choice of a pair of tongs over colourful clay toys that break by the time the children return home from a village fair. Hamid flaunts his purchase as a super toy by imagining it as capable of fulfilling various roles, but his grandmother is deeply touched when he tells her that he bought it for her. Hamid's resourceful and earthy imagination, and his gift of verbal and moral fight, resonate Gandhi's style that stirred India's imagination with unusual symbols like salt and khadi. They connoted a salvage archaeology aimed at reinventing a civilisation that had lost its soul.

It is no coincidence that children's literature in Hindi and several other Indian languages entered a prolonged spring in the 1930s. The range and quality of writing for small children published during the following two decades indicate a remarkable process of creative engagement with childhood. There were different kinds of elements in this surge. Experiment and debate over child upbringing and education were in the air. Gandhi's critique of schooling and his proposal for a radical version of pedagogic modernism should be seen in this larger context. Tagore and Gandhi made bold attempts to construct childhood with their distinct pedagogic visions and concerns. The bridge between their thoughts that Marjorie Sykes designed with her personal, interpretive effort is of rare significance for anyone interested in the history of a major discursive engagement with childhood.[1]

European history and thought resulted in the idea of an extended and protected childhood. We can distinguish two facets of this idea of protection. One was the physical protection of children from induction into work, the other was the protection of children from the knowledge of sexual good and evil—from the social practice of sexuality. The first resulted in the right of children to be compulsorily looked after, not merely by the family but by an institutional apparatus managed by the state. The other resulted in a notion of childhood as a period of sexual innocence coinciding with and extending to the psychological stage of latency. Many classics of European children's literature are steeped in this idea and portray the innocent adventures of children enjoying a long latency. For colonised nations like ours, the first aspect proved a difficult dilemma. The child's participation in the family's occupational life is a fact of rural life, both for the agricultural and the craft economy. It cannot be easily reconciled with the modern idea of prohibiting the child's involvement in income generation. The modern state is impelled by the urge to ban all forms of child labour so that every child can be schooled into citizenship. But child labour has persisted and is taking new forms, such as prostitution and domestic servitude in cities. Compulsory education, on the other hand, is struggling to acquire substance and meaning. The state has failed to impart dignity to the child's teacher, let alone the child.

The other modern parameter projects the idea of innocence. It means the child's isolation from sexuality during the years of latency, and from the practice of sexuality during adolescence. Modernity for Europe meant letting children be free from sexualised imagination so that they could exercise their freedom to grow into sexual beings at their own pace and with awareness. This second aspect of the European ideal of childhood has contributed to the recognition of latency as a significant period of intellectual growth. Freedom from sexual exploitation during childhood has proved far more elusive than freedom from participation in work. The global discourse of childhood, which was rooted in European thought and experience, has made us aware that the subject we are dealing with has many layers, specific to each society and its culture, and not just many dimensions. As one of the many societies in the world where child marriage was the norm barely three generations ago and still remains widely prevalent today, we need to recognise the struggle that the state and law face while coping with the power of culture. The law practises equity where there is no equality, so it is unable to deal with juvenile crimes in which girls are mostly the victim.

The study of gendering takes us to a frontier we wrongly assume to be familiar. The feminist movement and scholarship have amply demonstrated how incomplete and unbalanced the general knowledge of childhood is. At the same time, this radical development has given to many a sense of confidence that education will soon set the gender balance right. My own attempt to study the childhood of girls has led me to recognise that our optimism is unwarranted. In my book *Choori bazaar mein ladki* (2013), I presented a psycho-semiotic analysis of girls' childhood. It demonstrates the difficulties we face when we try to include girls in a general profile of childhood which is grounded in the idea and images of boyhood. Received or widely accepted knowledge in the area of child development suggests that a child's horizons widen as physical and intellectual capacities grow between the ages of five and eleven, that is, the primary school years. In the case of girls, the curtailing of physical movement begins precisely during these years, long before puberty sets in with its tougher regime. Body-centric consciousness and active denial of intellect are crucial aspects of the socialisation of girls in the family. Custom and ritual are implicated in the upbringing of girls in ways that have no parallel in the childhood of boys and which clash with the aims of education from the start of schooling. To think that the girl entering her school in her uniform leaves behind the girl who learns to live all aspects of her life in accordance with custom and ritual is to invite a fantasy to guide our analysis. Child marriage has statistically declined, but preparing a girl's mind to hold matrimony and motherhood as her highest goals remains common, everyday wisdom. These and numerous other aspects of gendering make a compelling case to say that our common construction of childhood is not compatible with girlhood.

Caste is another element that needs be taken into consideration in future attempts to study childhood in India. The recognition of the strength and resilience of caste as a social institution is yet to be applied to the study of caste as a powerful agency of socialisation during childhood. Leela Dube's analysis of gendering points towards the role that caste-specific customs and rituals might play in the early and later parts of girls' childhood. In the case of boys' acculturation into the caste system, there is some knowledge available in autobiographical literature. Autobiographies written by Dalit writers such as Om Prakash Valmiki are valuable sources of knowledge in the vast territory where the school encounters—or avoids—caste as a system that legitimises discriminatory practices. There is little doubt that the role of education as an agency of modernisation tends to be exaggerated when we assume that an educated person will be less caste-conscious. The same can be said about the role of urbanisation. Both such assumptions need to be questioned if the role of caste as a major agency of socialisation during childhood is to be fully comprehended. This line of questioning is necessary for childhood to evolve, in the long run, as a social category in India.

Before childhood could form and develop as a social category, with political recognition, a new unknown world overtook our imagination. This is the world of new information and communication technology. It has knocked down the boundaries within which Europe had tried to protect childhood. This field needs careful examination because it is so new and also because it is so firmly embedded in the political economy of footloose capital. Its impact on how human beings communicate and relate is being felt, but we do not know the full nature and consequence of this impact. How this impact is shaping adult–child relations is similarly unknown. The new technological environment blurs boundaries—between nation states, regions, cultures and generations. Children can now be directly accessed and inducted into a global community of consumer-citizens. All aspects of childhood, including play, are covered by this new community, which is managed by global conglomerates who design video games, toys and social media sites for children. Adults living in the immediate vicinity of the child are no longer the only or key agents of the child's socialisation. Parents can no longer play the role of protectors, nor can they set boundaries on the child's knowledge.

Like parents, the teacher too has less of a say in the new order. In the techno-romantic view, this is a moment of liberation of the child from adult control and supervision. Children are no more citizens in the making; the state intends to equip them for active membership of the global marketplace long before they avail all the rights associated with citizenship. The case of girls, once again, is somewhat different. In the global marketplace, they are of special interest because their powers and patterns of consumption are strongly linked to their own value as objects of consumption.

The new geography of the child's sphere of interaction makes older notions of protection and guidance meaningless. The child is back to being vulnerable in a world without boundaries. What this implies for the child's physical well-being and for intellectual and emotional development needs to be contemplated. For this contemplation, we have little guidance in the corpus of theory that has been available so far.

Note

1. For more information, see *Gandhi: His Gift of the Fight* (1987), by Jehangir P. Patel and Marjorie Sykes, published by Friends Rural Centre.

2

Education and Girlhood

This was the twenty-fourth J. P. Naik Memorial lecture delivered on 22 April 2016 at the Centre for Women's Development Studies, New Delhi.

It is a matter of honour and privilege for me to speak in the memory of J. P. Naik. The subject I will discuss was of great interest and concern to him. This lecture will take six turns in the course of about an hour. First, I will explain why I prefer to talk about girlhood rather than girls. Second, I will try to respond to the question, 'What is education?' At the third turn, we will briefly examine why knowledge requires an autonomous space. At the fourth turn, we will reflect on the psychological split in the state's mind in India. This will help us explain, at the fifth turn, the state's difficulty in engaging with culture, specifically the culture of girlhood. In the sixth and final turn, we will acknowledge the difficulties that the new age of assertive consumption presents for the education of girls. I will conclude by describing a gift given to a little girl by her father.

Why Girlhood?

I will talk about girlhood rather than girls. I have two interrelated reasons for this choice. One reason has to do with my understanding of girls' upbringing. The other has to do with the difficulties that the term 'childhood' presents when we use it to refer to girls. The considerable body of scholarship that now exists on girls' upbringing in India, and my own attempt to study this subject, have convinced me that the concept of socialisation does not convey the intensity of upbringing we notice in the context of girls. By 'intensity' I mean the determination with which social institutions, such as the family and kinship, act in order to mould a girl into a pre-sculpted model.

Leela Dube uses the term 'inescapability' while depicting one major dimension of a girl's preparation for the life destined for her as a woman (Dube 2001). The metaphor of metal casting comes to mind. What is known as the lost-wax method draws our attention to the malleability of wax that has been intricately crafted by expert hands to leave the exact marks of a chosen design on the clay that will serve, after it is fired, as a mould for metal casting. The term 'girlhood' refers to the culturally crafted mould used for imprinting the mind of the female child from the earliest stage of life. The idea of imprinting helps us to recognise the difficulties we might encounter if we use the term 'childhood' to describe the early part of a woman's life. It goes without saying that we are referring here to a pattern rather than to individual lives among whom one might notice many exceptions to the pattern.

To use the term 'childhood' for referring to this early stage of life invokes the normative meanings that childhood has acquired as a term. The historical trajectory of childhood as a concept refers to Europe since the eighteenth century, but its normative connotations have spread across the globe since mid-twentieth century (Kumar 2016). The normative attributes of childhood arise from the general theory of citizenship, and within it from the idea of child rights. The normative characterisation of childhood revolves around the idea of freedom, especially freedom from fear. Such an idea is hardly reconcilable with the pattern we notice when we attempt to study the everyday life of small girls. The cultural metallurgy I mentioned earlier ensures the internalisation of knowledge about the life that is exclusive to girls as children.

What is Education?

We will return to the subject of girlhood, but let us first talk about education and ask a question as direct as, 'What is education?' I will attempt an answer by using the corpus of knowledge that has developed over the twentieth century about the nature and growth of the human mind. Of course, this corpus of knowledge is not without debates and ambiguities, but it also includes vast areas of consensus, especially on matters like how children think and learn. On the basis of this consensus, we can give the following answer to the question, 'What is education?' Education is the means to obtain an entry into the social world while ensuring existence in the physical. 'Physical' and 'social' are not simply two dimensions of the milieu in which a child is born. Rather, they are two forms that the milieu takes. The key difference between them is that the physical milieu is visible or tangible while the social milieu is not. In its physical form, the milieu can be grasped by sensory means. But in its social form, the milieu waits to be discovered, and its discovery requires knowledge and skills. How the social milieu impinges on 'me' and 'my' life must be found out and understood by each child individually.

Why do the two milieux differ in this manner? The reason is that the physical milieu exists and is composed of elements that are living in the present, whereas the social milieu is composed of elements whose life is continuous with the past and merely touches the present. In other words, the constituents of the social milieu have been shaped by a past which borders the present. No one can see the past and the shaping that the social milieu went through in the past right up to the present moment in which the child stands. Only with the help of imagination—trained to notice and understand the shaping imparted to the social milieu in the past—can the child discover and grasp it. This is the task education must accomplish if it is education as distinct from socialisation. The latter term represents a process that facilitates the child's induction or entry into the social world so as to ensure adjustment to it. Socialisation takes place without making the mind specifically aware of the entry. Education, on the other hand, subjects the entry to all the demands that consciousness makes on cognition. The process of education can, thus, be expected to diminish the ineluctability of the social world by revealing to the learner's eye that the social world has a long past in which it evolved through human effort.

Tension between Home and School

This analysis points to a necessary tension between socialisation at home and education at school. While the home provides knowledge for the child's induction into the social world and adjustment to it, the school deals with different domains and kinds of knowledge, not necessarily consistent with the knowledge acquired at home from the family. While some kinds of knowledge acquired at school may promote acceptance, even appreciation, of the social world represented by the family, other kinds may undermine it and sow seeds of dissatisfaction and questioning, thereby undermining the family's role in preparing the child to adjust to the social world and its norms and values. We are not interested just now in the quality of education that a school might provide under the systemic conditions prevailing at a given time. We are referring to the school's nature as an institution to which society has assigned the task of enabling the young to access the knowledge available in different fields and also the related task of making it graspable. There are times when the curriculum carries the signs of having been designed to indoctrinate.

More usually, the different domains of knowledge or the subjects covered in the curriculum carry potentially contradictory messages or ideas that might unsettle young minds groomed at home. This is one reason why education sometimes has unanticipated consequences. The manner in which we defined education earlier suggests that the process of educating the imagination and intellectual energies of the young will attain its potential to the extent the school enjoys a certain degree of autonomy in its functioning. I am referring to autonomy in the manner by which knowledge is interpreted by teachers, the methods they use to teach and assess, and the resources of knowledge to which the school provides access. The greater the autonomy, the better the chance that the school will educate, in the sense indicated by our earlier discussion.

The State's Instinct and Role

In modern times, the school functions as an institution of the state. What kind of state a society has is a moot question, but all present-day societies seem to have delegated the task of educating the young to their states. If we look at the historical origins of the state in

India, we recognise the stamp of colonialism on it. As discussed in my work, *Politics of Education in Colonial India* (2014), colonialism is both an ideology and a set of practices. As an ideology, it entails a particular kind of relationship between rulers and the people over whom they rule. The colonial state apparatus was designed mainly to maintain law and order, and to speedily re-establish it when it broke down. This function continues to define the primary job of the Indian state even as other functions have emerged and accrued over time. These other functions arise from the value-framework of the Constitution, and are generative in their nature. As constitutional values, equality and justice have enabled the state to find new ways to perform its welfare role.

Between these generative functions and the older, dominant function, there is a gap. For this reason, the Indian state behaves as a psychologically split organism. Between its instincts and its consciously made choices, there is a sharp divide. The instinct is to control. This powerful instinct makes the state chronically apprehensive of the possibility that ordinary people might go out of control. The colonial perception that the majority of the 'native' population comprises the so-called masses exacerbates the state's apprehension of losing control. The conscious part of the state's personality is motivated by more benign feelings towards ordinary people and a differentiated image of the population. These feelings include the awareness that ordinary people are capable of behaving like responsible citizens. The idea of a citizen who has a stake in the state's functioning has acquired a kind of half-life: it drives the political side of democracy, while governance remains an exercise of control.

The state's difficulty in engaging with people's culture arises out of this split. History points to 1857 as the point when the colonial state decided to remain aloof when it came to cultural matters. Over the following ninety years preceding Independence, the colonial state handled social policy with restraint and caution. This meant that laws that deal with cultural practices like child marriage would remain vaguely worded and difficult to implement. The use of the term 'child' in the phrase 'child marriage' encrypts a wider tendency, not necessarily of colonial origin. This tendency is to equate boys with girls in the general consideration of being children, thereby overlooking the vast difference between the lived experience of the two sexes in the context of their social existence in the family and community in a matter like matrimony. The M. V. Joshi Committee (1928–29), which examined the consequences of child marriage, presented a vast amount of evidence, medical and other, demonstrating how marriage can be a painful and horrific experience for little girls (Rathbone 1934). We can hardly compare this experience with that of boys married away during childhood. The experience is not positive for them either, but in a different way. Gender neutrality of this law belongs to the wider phenomenon of the colonial state's sense of its own limitations. Colonial relations between the state and society implied a specific and studied caution in matters dealing with women. The public argument for this special caution was that women represent the core of culture. This perception allowed public policy to essentialise women's lives and matters pertaining to women. In effect, the state adopted the male perspective, leaving patriarchy undisturbed, to be reinforced in new forms under the regime of modernity. In education, the cautionary stance—towards matters designated as being culturally sensitive—meant the promotion of girl-specific curriculum policy. Strong continuity between home and school came to be regarded as a condition for the spread of girls' education. Under this approach, the school would do nothing that might weaken the norms, knowledge and self-identity cultivated through socialisation at home.

In our own day, the acceptance of this condition remains a tacit policy and a common perspective. Non-discrimination between boys and girls means overlooking the lives girls lead at home and the reality of their daily experience of negotiating the distance between home and school. The girl who attends school every day seems different from the one whose life at home is encircled by the customary demands of the family and community. The two girls inhabit the same body but they lead contrasting mental lives. The secular knowledge dispensed by the school to both boys and girls acquires a different set of meanings for the two sexes, reconstructed by their gendered selves so as to serve their culturally assigned roles in life. The assignment carries the force of imprinting on the girl's awareness that her body must serve as her primary agency both instrumentally and symbolically. What school knowledge might mean to a boy cannot be compared to what it might mean to a girl who has already internalised the culturally approved perceptions of the body's primacy and instrumentality.

Levels of Fear

Fear and preparedness for submission are deeply etched in socially sanctioned girlhood. Fear needs to be located in the broader mapping of the desirable female life to be lived under patriarchy. This broader perspective enables us to distinguish three levels of fear. In my book, *Choori bazaar mein ladki*, I have attempted to map an archaeology of fear in a girl's mind with the help of these three levels (Kumar 2013a). At the surface level, fear refers to the body in terms of injuries that might deface it. This is an important level for us to grasp. The consequences of such fear during infancy and early childhood needs to be considered, especially in the context of play. The power of play to absorb the young in the joy of the sheer physicality of the body loses its relevance if the parental gaze conveys an anxiety for the distant consequences of an injury caused by vigorous play. Girlhood means learning to be afraid of these consequences with reference to matrimony. Mahadevi Verma, in *Srinkhala ki kariyan* (1999), used the metaphor of merchandise to describe a girl's body. The merchandise must stay intact while it waits for a customer.

At the next level, fear covers sexuality. Internalisation of the fear of being violated takes many forms and requires the communicative gaze of the adult, but in this domain the gaze is surrounded and assisted by the vast and varied powers of mythology—its representation and celebration. The helplessness experienced by Draupadi or—under a different circumstantial sequence—Sita's ordeal are among powerful mythological depictions of fear that girls must internalise in their journey of growth towards becoming acceptable women. The mythical representation of fear covers both its importance and its management through acceptance of dependence on the male. This deep lesson is relevant to the third level of fear where it refers to independence and freedom. Fear of freedom ensures that the self is fully merged with socially given identities. As explored in Latika Gupta's *Education, Poverty and Gender* (2015), the absence or weak presence of a personal self has significant consequences for motivation to pursue and sustain personal goals.

These consequences of early or primary socialisation at home present a formidable problem for education. However, the problem never translates into a challenge. This is because the state, the custodian and manager of education, is historically conditioned to practise reluctance whenever it is required to engage with culture (Kumar 2010). For the state, equality between the sexes means a balanced presence of boys and girls in the classroom. Their differential experience of education is not even acknowledged in the state's own documents. In an arithmetical sense, equality has been achieved. In matters like curriculum, textbooks and teacher preparation, the state's policy has made a certain amount of effort to focus on girls, without addressing girlhood, that is, the culturally constructed life of girls. Neither male nor female teachers are equipped to deal with conflicts and contradictions that arise in the annual calendar of the school and its everyday life between educational aims and the aims of girlhood. While education implies the pursuit of aims chosen by a girl herself, girlhood means pursuing matrimony and motherhood as the highest aims of a woman's life. The school has little interest in a girl's life at home. By practicing neutrality or non-discrimination between boys and girls, the school overlooks the consequences of the lives they lead at home. It also ignores the layers of fear, including terror, sculpted in a girl's inner mental world by cultural imprinting through mythological and folk narratives, customs and rituals. The small number of girls who either escape this imprinting or manage to use their education to practise freedom quite often find themselves in the role of Abhimanyu, the young hero of Mahabharata who had to fight an all-round battle entirely by himself. Girls' education can take credit for producing a few thousand Abhimanyus who have symbolic, inspirational value for many others. For the vast majority, education creates a pleasant memory, of a time when, inside the walls of a school or college, freedom from terror could be experienced during the day.

New Alliance

This role of education may shrink and get tougher to perform in the foreseeable future on account of a growing alliance between custom and capital. This alliance between the market and culture is tightening its grip on girls' lives, thereby giving new strength to girlhood. Socialising the girl into an acceptable woman by facilitating her internalisation of the body project is a shared agenda of the market and custom. From the market side, partners include the various industries involved in the production of body merchandise and the electronic media where this merchandise is advertised and promoted. Television and cinema are also involved in the process of seeking girls' cooperation and active participation—by the exercise of her agency—in the body project. Assertive consumption of objects and services associated with the body reinforces the culture of girlhood. It is a travesty, not unusual for our times, that girls' co-option in the body project is interpreted in certain quarters as evidence of their agency.

The parents of a little girl who studies in a nursery have bought a dressing table to give her as a gift. She has learnt to use eyeliner and knows how to choose the right colour of lipstick to suit a dress. With peach-pink blusher on her cheeks, she preens as she looks at herself in the mirror. Her parents watch admiringly as she starts tottering towards them in her high-heeled shoes. Many of her classmates participated in similar attire in an annual event of her nursery. Their long educational journey has started.

REFERENCES

Dube, Leela. 2001. *Anthropological Explorations in Gender: Intersecting Fields.* New Delhi: Sage.

Gupta, Latika. 2015. *Education, Poverty and Gender.* New Delhi: Routledge.

Kumar, Krishna. 2013a. *Choori bazaar mein ladki*. New Delhi: Rajkamal Prakashan.

---. 2013b. 'Culture, State and Girls: An Educational Perspective.' *Economic and Political Weekly*, 45 (17): 75–84.

---. 2014. *Politics of Education in Colonial India*. New Delhi: Routledge.

Rathbone, Eleanor Florence. 1934. *Child Marriage: The Indian Minotaur*. London: George Allen and Unwin.

Verma, Mahadevi. 1999. *Srinkhala ki kariyan*. New Delhi: Rajkamal Prakashan.

3

Rurality, Modernity and Education

This paper is based on an address delivered on 12 August 2013 to mark the Foundation Day of the National University of Educational Planning and Administration in New Delhi.

As terms, 'modernity' and 'modernisation' are no more as popular in the scholarly world as they once were, but their use and relevance in the sphere of rural development and education have not diminished. Indeed, education and modernity are so tightly intertwined in our minds that neither can be thought of without referring, not necessarily by name, to the other. The concept of modernity has been associated with the recognition of individuality, freedom in the choice of occupation and the role of rationality in collective life (Rudolph and Rudolph 1967). Any attempt to define modernity will necessarily acknowledge the importance of education and universal literacy. Education is believed to intersect with modernity by way of its role in widening the horizons of awareness, by giving primacy to the individual, and by imparting skills and qualifications that enable the individual to exercise choice in the work market. It is not as if education creates modernity; rather, it embodies modernity inasmuch as its own encounter with modernity has transformed it so vitally. The pre-modern concept of education revolved around continuity and gave education the responsibility to perpetuate social norms. To be an educated person meant to personify social norms. The new or modern idea of education denotes individual freedom to an extent unthinkable at any time in the long history of education. To be educated in a modern sense implies the freedom to examine and question accepted norms.

Preference and Paradox

Modernity pervades our thinking about all major aspects of life, including where it is to be lived and how. Not surprisingly, urban living constitutes the leading edge of modernity. Large-size towns and cities symbolise modernity. Their growth, both in numbers and size, suggests that they are preferred by modern humanity as places of residence. The reasons for this preference are not difficult to guess. Material reasons are quite apparent, but psychological reasons are also important and relevant to the present discussion. Cities offer not just greater choice in the matter of occupation and opportunities for increase in income, but are also endowed with spaces, both real and symbolic, where the individual can hope to exercise his or her personal choices without the fear of interference. The anonymity of urban life is inconceivable in a rural setting. Life in a village is lived, not just metaphorically but literally too, under the gaze of other residents who comprise the community. Norms are observed with greater rigour, and choices that any individual member might exercise are limited. Living in a rural community demands constant speculation on the chances of approval for one's conduct by others. If an individual member questions the prevailing norms, it is highly unlikely that he or she will be tolerated with appreciation. The village community need not always be well knit in order to maintain its amorphous pressure over the conduct of an individual member.

The association of modernity with urban life poses a paradox for education because modernity in education is rooted in a pedagogic culture which is essentially rural. What we call 'progressive' pedagogy originated in the experiments and ideas of practitioners like Johann Heinrich Pestalozzi and John Dewey, whose worldviews were shaped by conditions of life in small rural communities. The America that shaped Dewey's mind and vision was a country of small communities surrounded by vast tracts of farmland and nature. His experimental pedagogy insists on every child being given the opportunity and freedom to explore things to their bare origins and to try out new ideas before accepting them. The importance of noticing natural phenomenon at first hand and to work out things backwards so as to comprehend where they originate are the kinds of advice that assume a rural setting. The common thread connecting many pedagogic pioneers, including Tagore and Gandhi, is the child's freedom and inventiveness—qualities necessary to make the best or most imaginative use of limited resources. Such a child would also be physically active in a familiar physical setting where it is possible to explore freely and confidently in a secure environment. Such a space invokes a village or small town, not a big city where the child's existence is constrained by dependence on transport, insecurity and parental anxiety. Life in the city also disallows going to the root of anything or makes this kind of pedagogic exploration difficult. Even an ordinary object like milk cannot be easily traced back to its origins except in pictures or words.

Modern Education under Colonial Rule

Let us now move to the universe of India's villages and place on record what we know about the recent history of teaching in a village school. Education in India is as old as India's civilisation, and up until the mid-nineteenth century, education denoted continuity. It served as the prime social agency for passing on knowledge, norms and values from one generation to the next. The changes that a prolonged intervention by colonial rulers in mid-nineteenth century brought about transformed the meaning of education and the character of the institutional order that imparted it. From being the conserver of tradition, education became the means for promoting and reinforcing changes in outlook, values and norms. This transformation of the idea and role of education occurred with the advent of the new system that colonial rulers introduced (Kumar 2014). The new system was oriented to the use of certified qualifications—acquired at a school or college—for the selection of men for state employment and professional careers. A new structure of rules, norms and incentives rapidly wiped out the older village schools that existed in several parts of India. Teachers who ran these village schools were dependent on the community, and the curriculum they followed addressed the needs and expectations embedded in village life. The new rules, curriculum design and incentives introduced by the colonial administration rendered the teachers working in indigenous schools redundant. For both the teacher and the community, the demise of the old system and the acceptance of the new one involved a deep change in attitudes towards education and the role of the teacher. This change was, of course, not isolated; it took place in the context of a new political economy based on radical changes in land ownership, growth in trade and commerce, and the rise of new classes and centres of power (Cohn 1987).

It is important to acknowledge that the new system of education was not altogether new. Though it marked a break from the older system in terms of its role in the larger economy, and state control over the curriculum, significant continuities persisted. The new curriculum was broader and its application in the classroom assumed a great deal of effort on the part of the teacher to arouse the child's interest. As Kazi Shahidullah specifically points out in *Patshalas into Schools* (1987), the curriculum introduced at the turn of the last century in Bengal was based on the new principles of pedagogy that were being applied at the time in Europe. However, the government could not set aside adequate financial allocations for the new curriculum to become a reality. Older practices like cramming and oral reproduction of memorised answers remained intact, and the new regime of examinations reinforced them. In any case, the popular perception that the foreign rulers were spreading alien knowledge in India undermined the community's confidence in the teacher's work and their own identification with the knowledge they were imparting. As education came to be seen as a means by which one could acquire certification, learning became subordinate to the selective function of education. The knowledge and skills that the new system offered had an instrumental value, in that their acquisition made the person think differently about themselves—as someone with the wherewithal to avail new opportunities (Walsh 1983). Those interested in pursuing the new opportunities coming up in towns and cities had no choice but to leave their ancestral village. The assumption that education displaces a person and changes not just his values and behaviour but also his place in the prevailing order gained popular currency in the context of the larger transformation of the economy. It is against this backdrop that we can comprehend the new grammar of rural–urban relations. The cultural transformation that took place in the nineteenth century shaped the perception that urban life represents the leading edge of modernity while rural life represents backwardness and resistance to modernity.

Grammar of Rural–Urban Relations

In the social and economic fluidity of colonial India, a rural habitation or village acquired the symbolic value of a place where a town-based educated man had come from. The opening question customarily used by Hindi-speaking strangers, '*Aap kahan ke rahne waley hein?*' (in approximate translation: 'Where are you from?') encapsulates the social history of the educated emigrant to the city. The city was the place *to* which a man *came* after obtaining some education; the village indicated the place where he had come *from*. Thus, the town or the city connoted aim or intended direction, whereas the village connoted a sacrificed belonging. These connotations formed a sign language in which the town signified the goal of one's struggle as an individual; the village signified the price one had to pay in terms of separation from the world into which one was born. Education signified the means or force fuelling mobility, both physical and social. It opened up new economic opportunities and pushed men towards a new status, causing the inevitable discomfort of separation from a familiar world characterised by a stable pattern of relations.

The idea that education enabled men to develop the disposition to seek new opportunities by leaving their familiar world behind also connoted new meanings for the town and the village as collectivities. These can be explored with the help of a grid (see Figure 1) wherein two layers of existential meaning, associated with the dimensions of time and space, have been distinguished. In terms of space, the

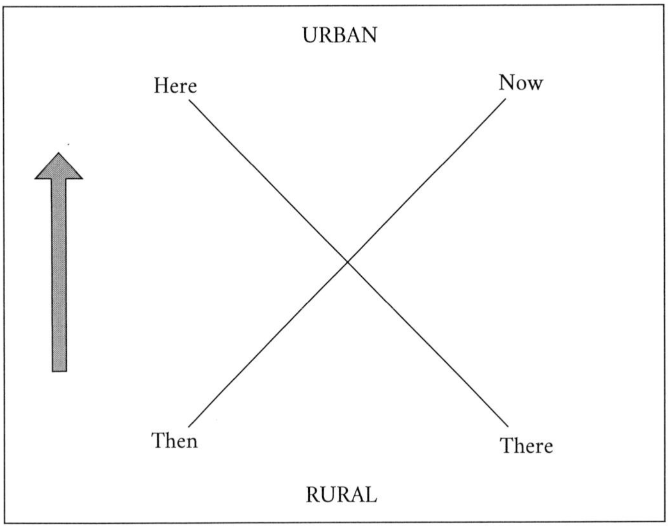

Figure 1: The urban and the rural in space and time

town or city suggests the place where a person is located in the 'now' of his life. He has left his own people behind in order to enter this new present, and he is not alone in doing this. The town, therefore, symbolises the 'now' of things in a larger, existential sense. It is the 'here' of discourse, in the sense that it represents the space where those who are discussing the world are situated. The phrase 'current affairs' captures this confluence of time and space that the town stands for in the lives of men who have struggled and made a common sacrifice that binds them. Their sacrifice consists of being cut asunder from a place that nurtured them as children and where their mothers lived. The relevance of such a place is in memory; it connotes a past one carries in one's mind, and a space to which one refers to distinguish the 'here' of the city. The village, on the other hand, stands for the 'then' and 'there' of life both in an individual and a collective sense.

This general grammar of rural–urban relations has a more specific epistemic dimension. The knowledge that now exists about the village in academic institutions and their libraries is the product of research or epistemic labour undertaken by a scholar who went to the village and stayed there for a length of time in order to collect reliable information about it. Such a scholar was either an anthropologist or an ancestor of the modern discipline of anthropology. As an officer serving the colonial administration, he carried out the difficult task of collecting first-hand information about the rural world when creation of knowledge about the countryside had become necessary for the colonial administration to consolidate its hold over the rural country. As Cohn pointed out, the study of the colonised has formed the subject matter of anthropology. He traces the modern view of the Indian village to the successive stages through which ideas, motives and methods of study passed from the late eighteenth century to the early twentieth century (Cohn 1987). For the colonial government, collection of revenue on a stable basis necessitated the study of older practices in land ownership and relations with the state. The prehistory of the modern decennial census that began in 1881 constitutes the growth of theory about village life, its culture and economy. From the idea of an isolated, self-sufficient republic to a political community with rigidly held values and norms, perceptions of the village were shaped by documentation and studies first undertaken by colonial officials. These perceptions influenced the modern view of Indian and, emblematically, Asian villages. 'The Victorian students of the Indian village were interested in the village as a type from which they could infer evolutionary stages and which could be used to compare similar developments or stages in other parts of the world'. The case of caste studies was similar, Cohn points out, as they 'reduced the need for specific knowledge' and allowed a general theory of rural life to emerge (Cohn 1987, 162).

Thus, beside the existential grammar of lived realities of emigrants, the town and the village are related to each other as epistemic entities in a parallel grammar of modernity. The town is where knowledge about the village is created and stored. Thereby, the village as an object of consciously and assiduously organised knowledge is born in the city. It is necessarily at a distance, indeed at a great distance in order to be adequately distinct. It is also deemed to represent a condition that is no more relevant and can only be tolerated in transition. Thirdly, its construction must represent the reverse of the city, its antonym. Stuck in this ultimate incompatibility, the village must be seen as being that which the city is not, and vice versa. For the village, there is just one way to liberate itself from this binding relationship, and that is to develop into a town according to the agenda of evolutionist modernity.

Rural Response to Modernity

With the advent of modern education under colonial conditions, rural–urban relations assumed a pedagogical nature. The city was now going to be the teacher and the village was going to be the learner. This distribution of roles essentially reincarnated the adult–child relationship in which colonial masters were cast as adults while natives were cast as children in need of education (Kumar 2014). The adult's responsibility involved an educative function. In the case of the coloniser, this educative function was to serve as a model of the rational man, representing the enlightenment ideals of Europe. This was the gist of the modernising role of colonial rule. It is explained with clarity in Lee-Warner's *The Citizen of India,* a civics textbook published in 1902 which was prescribed for a long time (Jain 2009). It presented the British Raj itself as the means whereby India will be educated. Rural–urban relations that developed under colonial rule entailed a similar educative function. They involved the transmission of modern ideas to the villager. The village-level worker was already a familiar functionary of rural development programmes in the early twentieth century (Moonaw 1939). His duties included imparting the knowledge of new agricultural practices to the peasants and making them aware of health-related problems.

As the century advanced and India achieved independence, the village-level worker became a key vehicle of rural modernity. The Community Development Programme undertaken in large parts of India in the early 1950s was a major initiative supported by state funds and external aid. Its aims were to bring about positive changes in rural India, including increase in land productivity, improving health standards and the spread of literary. Several accounts of this programme exist. I will draw upon S. C. Dube's *India's Changing Villages* (1958) and Kusum Nair's *Blossoms in the Dust* (1961). Both these studies offer valuable insights into the conditions that prevailed in villages in the 1950s and how they responded to the Community Development Programme. An interesting item mentioned by both Dube and Nair is the introduction of compost making as a way to improve conventional waste-disposal practices and harness waste for making manure. Dube reports that the compost pits in the villages where the team of researchers went were lying empty. When inquiries were made why this was so, the respondents explained that the idea of making compost was good but impractical because upper-caste women could hardly be expected to walk through the village to its outskirts, carrying waste and cow dung. Nor could men do this because it was considered women's work. And no one could afford servants. Dube includes this explanation among the cultural factors that any process of induced social change must take into account. Compost making also figures in Nair's account of village life in western Uttar Pradesh and Punjab during the late 1950s. She found empty compost pits in many upper-caste villages of western Uttar Pradesh. They had been abandoned because the upper-caste villagers could not touch the refuse material with their hands. A low-caste woman (bhangin) engaged by them threw it in a pile at the village border. Residents of a village in Saharanpur told Nair: 'To our shame we have to admit that we do not make good quality compost simply because our lands are at some distance from the village and the bhangin will not carry the refuse so far. She simply throws it in a heap near the road and the rain washes away most of it' (Nair 1961, 110).

Nair's narrative throws rare light on rural response to new ideas. The expectation had been that such ideas would be appreciated for their inherent worth and swiftly adopted. What actually happened seems to have surprised and disappointed those who believed that rural progress depended on the diffusion of new techniques and their adoption. The cultural terrain turned out to be both complex and resistant. Both Nair and Dube suggest that a great deal had already changed in India as a result of new legal and institutional provisions, but they also acknowledge the continuation of resistance to such changes. Dube attributes some of this resistance to an insufficient concern for cultural factors in the planning of strategies aimed at rural modernisation (Dube 1958).

We can extend this discussion to formal education. The educated son of a peasant who does not want to work in the farm is a proverbial example of the negative effect of modern education on young rural minds. We need to examine this proverbial wisdom somewhat critically if we want to come to terms with rural response to modernity. Indeed, the explanation is not unknown or new, though it may appear to be so to educational planners. Nair reflects briefly on education towards the end of her book. Exploring the apparent incompatibility between education and farm life, beyond the physical challenge it involves, she says: 'There is also the fact to consider that within the village the individual is never detached and thrown into new and different surroundings of *abstract and impersonal relationships which can be expected to emancipate him and compel his transformation, distorted or otherwise*, as happens when he moves into an industrial area of a large city' (Nair 1961, 196; emphasis added). The point Nair is making has found corroboration in studies of village society and its literary representation. Education, especially when it is prolonged and successful, brings about both eligibility for alternative forms of occupation and higher income; it also creates self-consciousness. For both these reasons, it disturbs the equilibrium associated with the culture of everyday life in a caste-based structure of social relations.

Education implies occupational diversity within a group and change in the lifestyle and status of individual families. The educated son of a small-scale peasant or a landless labourer who prefers to move to a city is usually cited as an instance of the displacement effect of the kind of education that is irrelevant to village life. However, the origin of this desire to migrate may be more complex. As Miller points out in *From Hierarchy to Stratification* (1975), such cases may, in fact, exemplify escape from a situation that an educated son of a landless labourer cannot hope to change. Modernisation of the village economy has created some new opportunities in the village too, but availing oneself of these opportunities requires a lot more than mere education. Any opportunity that offers higher income and change in status, through employment or contract jobs, also brings with it the challenge of renegotiating the established framework of dominance. In such a challenge, education is of no use. As Beteille points out in 'Ideas and Interests' (1969), control over land, capital and labour determines who takes advantage of the new opportunities that arise in the village itself. Those who have nothing but education to help them must go elsewhere, that is, to a city or town, to seek a better life. In other words, they must escape from the village.

New Realities

Over the last half century, rural India has gone through significant processes marking a change in its size and proportion in the total population, its economic condition and its education. Let us examine what these changes might mean in terms of rural modernity. While the overall size of the rural population has been rising, the proportion of the population residing in rural areas has been steadily declining. As Table 1 shows, the proportion of India's rural population steadily declined throughout the twentieth century, but the decline has somewhat accelerated since 1971.

Table 1: Size and proportion of rural population during the twentieth century (collated from census figures)

Year	*Size of rural population (in millions)*	*Proportion of total population*
1901	213	89.2
1911	226	89.7
1921	223	88.8
1931	246	88.0
1941	275	86.1
1951	299	82.7
1961	360	82.0
1971	439	80.1
1981	524	76.7
1991	629	74.3
2001	743	72.2

This decline is mirrored in the steady rise of the urban population, especially that of metropolitan cities and provincial capitals. This demographic fact is commonly explained by changes since the 1970s that have influenced the rural economy and its place in the overall national economy. These changes point to the growing political dominance of the urban-industrial sector and the diminishing recognition of the economic role that agriculture and related occupations play. Economic changes also include the loss of village commons, such as pasture land, local forests and ponds, which used to sustain the poorer sections of the rural population.

But, perhaps more important than all of these is the general pull that urban life and the advantages it offers have exercised on the rural population. The mass media have also strengthened this pull by giving both exposure and popularity to urban norms and standards, both economic and social, not necessarily in an unbiased or realistic manner. Guha, in *India After Gandhi* (2006), includes this last factor in the list of economic and social factors that might have contributed to the phenomenon of farmer suicides, which has occurred during the last three decades at a rate unprecedented in the long history of the peasantry. It is indicative of the larger rural crisis that has manifested in several other symptoms. No symptom is as dramatic or as worrisome as that of the rise in extremism in approximately one-third of India's districts. These are concentrated in eastern-central India, covering the tribal belt of Bengal, Jharkhand, Orissa, Madhya Pradesh, Andhra Pradesh and Maharashtra. The conflict and civil strife endemic to certain parts of these states has affected all aspects of the life of rural residents, including the education of their children.

In the context of education itself, the period following the 1960s has been quite significant for rural India. The big story, so to say, is that of the momentum that the state's attempt to universalise elementary education acquired from the late 1980s onwards. This momentum was reflected first in the District Primary Education Programme (DPEP) and then in the Sarva Shiksha Abhiyan (SSA). As a consequence of such momentum, and the general social trend towards literacy, more men and women in rural India now possess the rudimentary skills associated with literacy than was the case at any earlier point in modern history. As a characteristic of modernity, literacy serves as an important indicator of people's capacity to participate in democratic procedures and civic interaction. The spread of literacy can also be seen in the context of the seventy-third amendment of the Indian Constitution, under which elected panchayats now represent a means of local self-governance. This amendment has had special implications for rural education because the running of primary schools is one of many responsibilities which falls under the purview of the village panchayat. Lastly, there is the Right to Education Act under which every child between the ages of six and fourteen is entitled to a free education. Along with the mid-day meal scheme, this provision of a right to elementary education completes the broad picture of the factors of change introduced by the state in rural India. The question we can now consider is: How might these policy changes and legal reforms shape our perception of rural modernity?

Our capacity to answer this question depends on the accuracy with which we can interpret these policy-related measures, bearing in mind the economic and sociocultural information we have about rural India. We also need to remember that education is one of the prime means through which the grammar of rural–urban relations, discussed earlier, has been internalised by successive generations of the rural population. Education is thus not only a measure of modernity but is also a designer of modernity's inner nature and meaning. In education, modernity implies commitment to equality and acceptance of individual differences among children. It is difficult to summarise the role of education in India due to the vast sociocultural differences that exist between the southern states, where the roles of the state and the market are better reconciled, and the northern states, where the rural economy is poorly served by both. However, looking at the broader picture, there are significant pan-Indian continuities in terms of endemic problems such as gender and caste-based disparities in literacy, employment and children's education. In *Rural India Facing the 21st Century* (2002), Harriss-White and S. Janakarajan present an elaborate analysis of how these disparities directly influence the chances that individual children might have of availing education. The social contours of these disparities may differ from region to region, but their persistent presence is irrefutable. Government reports tend to rely on enrolment data to emphasise how the gender gap has been bridged, while ignoring the length of girls' education and the quality of their experience at school. The minimalist nature of special programmes for rural girls, some of which are indeed innovative and effective, has been highlighted in 'What is Missing in Girls' Empowerment' (Kumar and Gupta 2008) in the analysis of the Kasturba Gandhi Balika Vidyalaya (KGBV) scheme. A similar critique is applicable to the manner in which caste-related disparities have been addressed. Better representation of the lower-caste groups in textbooks is one thing, empathetic and professional handling of mixed-caste classrooms by teachers is quite another. Ironically, the same programmes that pushed enrolment up have also diluted the village teacher's economic status and professional identity.

Conclusion

Rural education has been conceptualised and defined over the last two centuries as a means of uplifting and reconstructing village society. This vision necessarily implies a benevolent agency external to the rural world. It is hardly surprising that the implementation and outcome of this vision have exacerbated the dependent status of the village, both economically and culturally. The city sets the norms, the village attempts to follow them. Established curriculum and pedagogy reflect this vision and translate it into the socialisation of mind and behaviour. In terms of this vision, modernity consists of the preparedness of the rural child for adjustment in an urban environment. This vision denies any possibility of authentic existence to an educated person in a rural setting. The term 'authentic' here is meant to convey the sense in which Taylor uses it in *The Malaise of Modernity* (1991) to convey personal standards of rationality and moral judgement. An educated rural person who chooses to stay in the village is likely to be perceived as being irrational, given the pervasive dominance of the vision of rural education embedded in the state's policies.

The other side of rural education needs to be considered too, before we deliver too harsh a judgement. As a seat of caste-based relationships and land-centred structures of dominance, the village can hardly offer a hospitable ethos to a person educated for a sustained length of time. The changes in a person's outlook, behaviour and level of awareness as a result of education, and the concomitant changes in lifestyle, can make life rather difficult in an ethos shaped by an ineluctable acceptance of caste and gender hierarchies and group dominance. Education makes a person unfit for adjustment to such an ethos unless a substantial amount of curricular designing and pedagogic attention is focused on mollifying the ethos itself. In the history of modern Indian education—both under colonial rule and self-governance—the curriculum has primarily served as a means of dissemination and control through prescribed textbooks, fixed examinations and ensuring that a teacher's status is not well regarded. As a vehicle of modernity, education remained largely empty of modern pedagogic values such as child-centredness and engagement with the child's milieu. Attempts made during the colonial period to modernise pedagogy and curriculum did not receive adequate financial backing, and this has remained the case in the post-Independence period. Even at present, when the curriculum has opened up to the possibility of including critical pedagogy as an objective of learning (NCERT 2006), the state is not prepared to recognise and appreciate the agency of rural teachers. In the second decade of the twenty-first century, the state is keener to invest in the free distribution of laptops among rural youth than in teachers' emoluments, well-being and professional training. The great potential that rural schools have for the practice of pedagogic modernism, discussed at the beginning of this paper, remains untapped.

For any fresh vision of rural modernity and education to emerge, it will be important to look back and explore more deeply the period in which rural India encountered modernity under colonial conditions. For instance, while we know that colonial rule had devastating consequences for India's crafts, especially weaving, knowledge about the consequences of land-control laws introduced during colonial rule is neither sufficiently differentiated to cover all parts of India, nor is it socially deep enough to explain how different classes and communities were affected. Rural communities dependent on forests faced and continue to face a difficult struggle. While there is no single picture that can represent all regions of a country as diverse as India, a certain amount of truth seems to reside in the impression that rural life and its perception went through radical change. As Saurabh Dube puts it in 'Lost and Found' (2010), as an object of knowledge and curiosity, the village has been repeatedly discovered and lost in recent history. On a visit to a village school, one cannot miss the tragic implications of the teacher's lowly status and poor-quality training.

The idea of the unchanging Indian village was proved to be a myth a long time ago, but the village we construct with our modern, urban imagination is at least partly a myth of our own making. The point Raymond Williams makes in the context of England is equally true of India—namely, that although the country and the city convey two contrasting types of reality, our real experience of them is not of two singular forms, but of 'many kinds of intermediate and new social forms of social and physical organization' (Williams 1973, 289). Urban educators can hardly ignore their impact, and the impact of their predecessors, on the manner in which 'rural' is conceptualised, and on different aspects of life in real villages, especially the education of children who grow up there. One contribution of modern education and its curriculum has been to reinforce a polarity between rural and urban living. Such a polarity hardens prevailing stereotypes by projecting on to the village what the city has supposedly left behind. The real-life experience of both villagers and city-dwellers may offer far greater evidence of an overlap than a polarity. The insistence that the remaining agenda of modernity is mainly in villages often leads to distorted priorities. Many well-placed modernisers today convey an unmistakable impatience with rural problems. They offer technical solutions for quick, radical effect. Such men rarely have the historical sense to recall how resilient the Indian village has proved in its long history.

REFERENCES

Beteille, Andre. 1969. 'Ideas and Interests: Some Conceptual Problems in the Study of Social Stratification in Rural India.' *International Social Science Journal* 21(2): 219–34.

Cohn, Bernard S. 1987. *An Anthropologist among the Historians and Other Essays*. Delhi: Oxford University Press.

Dube, Saurabh. 2010. 'Lost and Found: Villages between Anthropology and History.' In *Village Matters*, edited by Diane P. Mines and Nicholas Yazgi, 31–50. Delhi: Oxford University Press.

Dube, Shyama Charan. 1958. *India's Changing Villages*. London: Routledge and Kegan Paul.

Guha, Ramachandra. 2006. *India After Gandhi*. London: Pan Macmillan.

Harriss-White, Barbara, and S. Janakarajan. 2002. *Rural India Facing the 21st Century: Essays on Long-Term Village Change and Recent Development Policy*. London: Anthem Press.

Jain, Manish. 2009. 'Civics Curriculum and the Idea of Citizen.' (PhD, University of Delhi).

Kumar, Krishna. 2014. *Politics of Education in Colonial India*. New Delhi: Routledge.

Kumar, Krishna, and Latika Gupta. 2008. 'What is Missing in Girls' Empowerment?' *Economic and Political Weekly*, 43(26–27): 19–24.

Miller, D. B. 1975. *From Hierarchy to Stratification: Changing Patterns of Social Inequality in a North Indian Village*. Delhi: Oxford University Press.

Moomaw, I. W. 1939. *Education and Village Improvement*. London: Oxford University Press.

Nair, Kusum. 1961. *Blossoms in the Dust: The Human Factor in Indian Development*. London: Gerald Duckworth.

NCERT. 2006. *National Curriculum Framework 2005*. New Delhi: NCERT.

Rudolph, Lloyd I., and Susanne Hoeber Rudolph. 1967. *The Modernity of Tradition*. Chicago: University of Chicago Press.

Shahidullah, Kazi. 1987. *Patshalas into Schools: The Development of Indigenous Elementary Education in Bengal, 1854–1905*. Calcutta: Firma KLM.

Taylor, Charles. 1991. *The Malaise of Modernity*. Toronto: House of Anansi Press.

Walsh, Judith E. 1983. *Growing Up in British India: Indian Autobiographers on Childhood and Education under the Raj*. New York: Holmes and Meier.

Williams, Raymond. 1973. *The Country and the City*. London: Chatto and Windus.

4

The Logic of Children's Right to Education

The law on Right to Education (RTE) carries the legacy of Article 45 and reminds us of its long struggle to achieve universalisation of elementary education. Article 45 carried a *directive principle* of state policy. While the directive principles given under Part IV of the Constitution are important, they cannot be enforced by the judiciary. Hence, the failure of Article 45 to achieve its purpose reminds us of the state's capacity to direct itself towards a constitutional goal. The new Article 21-A, which RTE attempts to implement, calls for reflection on the long trial of Article 45 and the factors that made it ineffective. To say that the state did not make a sincere effort to implement Article 45 would mean attributing motive to failure. Such an attribution is never easy to prove. Also, it will stop us from examining the nature of the progress made towards achieving universal elementary education; initially made in the 1950s and then, after a gap, in the 1990s. If RTE is to perform better than Article 45 did, the policy and the methodology followed by the state, and the social constraints it faces, will need to be recalled. The soft approach to child labour, reflected in the Constitution itself (for example, in its distinction between hazardous and non-hazardous labour), exemplifies the force of social constraints the state faces. Child marriage presents a similar case, illustrating the role of culture in shaping the state's accommodative disposition. We can anticipate the implementation of RTE to be hampered by these familiar constraints under contemporary historical conditions.

Childhood continues to be perceived mainly and merely as one stage of life, and responsibility towards children is recognised as a social value governing the conduct of adults towards their own progeny in the context of family and kinship. Children are yet to emerge in India as an important social category, occupying a distinct space in the collective consciousness of society. As many scholars have pointed out, girls are specifically valued for their capacity to procreate, and their intellectual potential and contribution are regarded as being relevant only in exceptional cases. The new economic regime of neo-liberalism has accentuated the role of girls and women as relievers of male tedium, and as enhancers of entertainment. Their use in Indian Premier League cricket is a case in point. RTE's discourse jars with these perceptual and material contemporary realities. The new chapter RTE has opened in the social and legal history of childhood promises to be full of struggle and resistance.

At this juncture, it is necessary for us to distinguish RTE from other fundamental rights granted by the Constitution. A key distinction arises from the fact that RTE imparts a right to someone who cannot secure it without assistance and who cannot protest or fight for it if it is denied or violated. There are limits to child activism, especially at the start of the age span RTE covers. Moreover, denial of RTE during the relevant age span cannot be compensated for at a later stage. This is because the opportunity to be educated shapes the nature of childhood one would have, and also because childhood constitutes an opportune time to be educated. RTE has a unique place among fundamental rights as its fulfilment depends on the collective conscience of adult society. However, it resembles all other rights in one crucial respect. Any right can be said to be in good shape only so long as it does not need to be asserted. It is advantageous to have a right only if the 'other', that is, someone who has the power to deny it, is aware of it and respects it. For instance, if a woman has a right to dignity, her assertion of this right would imply that either she apprehends its violation or that the violation has already occurred. If a right fails to arouse a sense of duty in the 'other' to respect it, then the right has little value, except as a basis for protest. In the case of RTE, protest after its denial would have little meaning because childhood cannot be relived.

Promulgation of RTE forms a reluctant start to the acceptance of children as a legal and moral responsibility of the social collective and the state. A verdict given by the Supreme Court in 2012, which upheld the constitutional validity of RTE, underlines this joint ownership. Certain questions remain to be settled, especially in relation to the professional status and preparedness of the person charged with the task of fulfilling the responsibility on behalf of society and state. For historical reasons, teachers who work with children lack social and economic status, and their training lacks professional rigour. RTE requires a new kind of teacher who does not merely follow the prescribed textbook but actively shapes the intellectual life of a mixed classroom with children from diverse backgrounds and exercises personal judgement to take decisions when required. Teachers' working conditions, both in state-run and private schools, will have to change quite radically if RTE's vision is to become a reality in the foreseeable future. The debates surrounding RTE do not indicate adequate appreciation of its vision. The court case[1] fought on behalf of private schools suggests their inability to recognise the new curricular and pedagogic philosophy underlying RTE. On the other hand, short-term solutions typically sought by state governments, especially in the north, to overcome the chronic shortage of teachers indicate a concern for formal compliance as opposed to commitment. Similarly, the permission granted to resume the pass–fail system signifies systemic impatience with RTE's vision. Even if RTE marks a turning point in the story of universalisation of elementary education in India, the road beyond will neither be short nor smooth.

Following the Supreme Court's ratification of RTE in 2012, RTE's future now depends on teachers. When I said this to a friend who teaches in a primary school, she said, 'You are being unfair.' I was startled to hear that response because what I had said was common sense. When I pointed this out to her, she said, 'Common sense isn't enough to implement RTE—you need professional insight, so you need policies that allow teachers to develop insight and use it.' She is right. For well over a century, India has treated its teachers like messengers who need not know or understand the message themselves. They occupy the lowest rung in the ladder of authority and status in the system of education. The younger the age group they teach, the lower their own status and salary. That is why the nursery teacher has no status at all, and few university-level training courses exist for them—which might explain *why* certain practices are good and others are bad. Primary-level teaching is similarly regarded as a drill devoid of intellectual effort. Delhi University stuck its neck out by offering a four-year course called Bachelor of Elementary Education. Though it has produced outstanding teachers for more than a decade, the Delhi government still denies them the status of trained graduate teachers. In its recent verdict, the Supreme Court characterised education 'as a process involving many actors', starting the list with 'the one who provides education', namely, the teacher. The list then goes on to include the owners of institutions, parents, the child, society and the state. This clarity of analysis runs through the entire verdict, which should become compulsory reading for administrators and teachers alike if RTE is to reach its ambitious goals.

Most ambitious among its objectives is the social engineering it proposes by guaranteeing at least twenty five per cent share of enrolment in unaided fee-charging schools to children whose parents cannot afford to pay the fees. This provision was the focus of the petition that the Supreme Court has disposed of with its majority verdict. The petitioners had challenged the provision arguing that reserving twenty-five per cent of seats, that too without screening, implies an unwarranted curtailing of the autonomy of an unaided private institution. The analysis used by the Supreme Court to reject this argument is both complex and sharp, basically showing why the right to run a private school is not absolute. The Supreme Court's logic is that Article 21A has come into being because certain Directive Principles, particularly Article 45, required the state to provide *for* free and compulsory education for all children up to the age of fourteen. The proposition *for* is important, says the verdict, because it is in response to the Directive Principle that the new law has established the manner in which the state has decided to follow the principle. The chosen manner covers both state and private schools. The verdict also reminds us that RTE has been woven into the Right to Life, on the grounds that a life worth living must have dignity and that is what education promises to impart. Secondly, the new law, and the right coded in this law, concerns children, and not institutions. Thirdly, RTE also covers quality as an aspect of education, not something external to it. The state has now fully admitted to being a custodian of all children, so it has a right to impart recognition to institutions providing education in the manner stipulated by law or withdraw recognition from institutions that are not doing so.

This is as clear as it can be. Yet, one can understand why private schools are upset and startled. One simple reason is habit. Unaided schools have been used to thinking that they can isolate the children under their care from the poverty, roughness and pain of daily life that surrounds prosperous Indians. The belief that learning needs withdrawal from the jungle of life has a long, very long history. In the history of pedagogic theory, this view was challenged more than a century ago. In Europe and America, experience was recognised as the best teacher at the beginning of the twentieth century, and experience includes direct exposure to the diversity of the human condition. Mixed schooling took a while to take root, and in the US it had to await the pressure generated by the civil rights movement. Indian private schools, including the elite among them, are startled that they are coming under a law they did not help to formulate. These schools have been used to seeing themselves as leaders. Their teachers are accustomed to working with a select group of children whose home environment is homogenous. Now, these teachers will have to cope with a mixed classroom. They will have to learn and practise new pedagogies capable of maintaining high standards in the face of India's sociocultural diversity and economic disparity. The crucial lesson they have to learn now is that the inclusion of children belonging to the poorer sections of society and marginalised groups is not just good for them, but also for the remaining seventy-five per cent. This is so because classroom life will now be experientially and linguistically richer. It will be easier to illustrate complex issues with examples drawn from children's own lives. In the syllabi and textbooks developed in the wake of the National Curriculum Framework (2005), all subjects, not just the social sciences, require understanding from diverse perspectives. Peer-group learning is as important as what the teacher teaches. Indeed, the teacher's job is to nurture a classroom culture which enables children to take interest in differences of opinion, perceptions and lifestyle, in order to bring life and learning closer together.

However, the owners of unaided institutions are going to perceive their critical challenge in finances. They want to know where the funds for the free seats are going to come from. RTE stipulates that the state will subsidise the cost of reserved seats by paying private schools an amount representing the per-child expenditure the state incurs in its own schools. Schools charging a high fee argue that this amount is just not sufficient to cover the expenses that the school incurs for maintaining its quality. This argument needs to be examined with care as it contradicts the popular theory that state-run schools are of poor quality because their teachers are unaccountable. By describing the state's compensation for free seats as inadequate, the unaided private schools are conceding the point that the quality of education in state schools is hampered by paucity of funds. In order to substantiate their claim to greater efficiency, private schools must now show better outcomes with the same amount of funds per child that the state spends in its own schools. Indeed, this may provide to private schools an opportunity to set their own priorities in order. Over the last few decades, a culture of extravagance has engulfed many of India's elite private schools. From expensive furniture and marble floors to air conditioning and CCTVs, many private schools now uninhibitedly flaunt their five-star luxuries. When you visit one of these schools, you wonder whether you are in a hotel. Their plea for sympathy over the inadequacy of state subsidy for twenty-five per cent free seats is a bit tedious.

They should shift their anxiety to the challenges that RTE throws at everyone concerned with children's education—teachers, trainers, parents, state and society. For teachers, the critical issue is to absorb the new curricular and pedagogic perspective which focuses on learning in place of marks. RTE asks for continuous and comprehensive evaluation, and a ban on corporal punishment and private tuition. These are tall demands and our systemic preparation to meet them has barely begun. A search for short cuts is an ominous sign which is already visible in the choice of distance education for teacher training and dependence on NGOs for monitoring. The RTE Act has assigned the monitoring of implementation to the National Commission for the Protection of Child Rights (NCPCR). Currently, this fragile agency has hardly any institutional capacity to look after the millions of children whose right to education and dignity has been recognised for the first time in the nation's history. Help from non-government organisations can hardly substitute a workforce of academic and legal specialists that NCPCR and its state units across the country require. The verdict delivered by the Supreme Court puts the onus for the execution of RTE on the entire society and the apparatus of the state.

NOTE

1. Society for Un-aided private schools of Rajasthan vs. the Union of India, 2012.

5

Regimentation and Nationalism

This essay is excerpted from 'Can Education Contribute to Peace?', published by MGIEP (UNESCO) in 2018.

Two decades ago, I went through an experience which convinced me of how necessary peace education was. In 1998 I started a study of the textbooks used in India and Pakistan for the teaching of history. My study was confined to the portrayal of the anti-colonial or nationalist struggle. This was a segment of the past that the two modern nations had shared until Partition in 1947. My interest was in examining how the ninety-year period, from 1857—when the British faced the first major rebellion—to Independence and Partition in 1947, is discussed in a sample of mainstream[1] textbooks used in the two countries. After a preliminary analysis of the textbooks, I decided to visit Pakistan and chose to travel by the Delhi–Lahore bus that had recently been introduced as a symbol of the shared aspiration of the two governments to improve bilateral relations. Hostility between the two nations had been interrupted several times earlier by similar symbolic gestures, without attaining sustainable peace. The bus left New Delhi early in the morning and took the whole day to reach Wagah, where the Indo–Pak border provides an official passage for traffic from both sides. Checking of passports and luggage took a long time before I could board the bus along with other passengers. As soon as the bus started, I noticed a group of small boys playing cricket in a nearby vacant plot of land. This was a common, familiar sight. However, at the moment of seeing those boys, I was struck by the thought that their minds carried a very different construction of the past and the present. The role education had played in giving them, as Pakistanis, and me as an Indian, two different designs of knowledge about the past became clear in that moment. That this is the role whereby education contributes to the hostility between the two nations became clear in that epiphanic moment.

National borders all over the world serve as epistemic watersheds, though not in every case do they separate historical constructions as sharply divergent as those of India and Pakistan. Borders between nations mark the modern state's role in deciding what the young will learn in order to belong to the nation located within those borders. The state uses its authority to calibrate the kind of belonging schools will nurture towards the nation and also the intensity of the sense of belonging.

Education and Indo–Pak Hostility

In many countries, religion and its history as a social institution are intertwined with the history of modern nationalism. This condition appears to have been responsible for hostility and war-like relations between nation states in recent times. The case of India and Pakistan is of this kind although there are several factors that make their mutual hostility look like a somewhat unique matter. At the same time, there are factors that lend to their hostile relationship a rather common character of territorial rivalry. For educational planners, especially curriculum designers, study of Indo–Pak history offers an important lesson, namely, that education cannot be seen in isolation from the wider ethos of society. This lesson has value for curriculum planners concerned about peace in any part of the world. The depth at which sedimented layers of knowledge about the past influence learning at school requires recognition for any significant attempt to reorient education towards peace to succeed. While it is true that the Indo–Pak problem cannot be reduced to a single or simple axis, religion and its relationship with the growth of nationalism have a definite explanatory value for making sense of the problem. And it does not arise from the Indo–Pak partition alone as many would like to believe. Had undivided India not been partitioned in 1947 along religious lines by the departing British colonial authorities, religious strife between the two major religious identities of the region would still have remained a live phenomenon. It had already become one in the latter half of the nineteenth century. The widely held view that the Hindu–Muslim divide was stoked by the colonial rulers in their own interest is of course true, but it is only a half-truth. The advent of modernity and its expression in political institutions and procedures provide us with the other half.

Colonial authority furnished an axis along which the two religious identities struggled with modern institutions, such as the census, courts, schools and the elections for representation at various levels (Cohn 1987). Religious identity provided an available resource that the elites, both colonial and local, could use to negotiate the emerging structure of economic and political opportunities. They used religious identity, wound up as it was in history, legend and myth, to mobilise popular support in order to strengthen their clout in engaging with the British colonial power structure. With the passage of time, the engagement grew into full-scale politics. Contrary forces also emerged, challenging the use of religion as a political tool. However, religion did remain a crucial handle for the colonial government to deal with contending claims, creating copious opportunities for taking advantage of the religious divide.

Following Partition, India and Pakistan became two separate national entities with their own states articulating their national spirits. Once the separation occurred, the two entities acquired great mutual reactiveness (Kumar 2007). Any observer who attempts to understand the negative energy that flows between the two entities is likely to assume that their internal worlds are entirely different. The self-identities the two nations publicly carry do indeed look different. India carries the self-identity of a secular nation state where people of different religious faiths live with constitutionally endowed equal rights. Pakistan, on the other hand, carries the self-identity of a state based on Islam with the intent of practicing Islamic values in all domains of life, including politics and civil administration. These two distinct, official self-identities interact on the global or public stage as fixed role players or actors in a symbolic play. The plot in which the two nations serve as characters in the play is historical, drawing its causality from the pre-Partition past and moving towards a known, logically coherent future. We can call it a story of two nationalisms, exuding incompatibility in an extended competition for claim to moral superiority.

Claim to the moral higher ground is the heart of the message conveyed to the young in the two countries. Both the Indian and the Pakistani narratives of the history of the freedom movement attempt to convince the young that as modern nation states, they have a principled reason to be different in an incompatible way. This objective of the narratives is grounded in the need to explain why Partition occurred, both as an event by itself and as the defining moment of freedom from colonial rule. If the two narratives offered instances of similarity between the two nations, how would Partition find a sufficient justification? This structural imperative compels them to be as divergent as possible. Since the two nations have a shared past, the historians who prepare textbooks must construct the past differently, placing all major events in a light capable of rendering it different from how it might look to the other nation.

Divergence is also attained with the help of characterisation, especially that of heroes or great leaders. Their portrayal as influential, larger-than-life personalities enables the two narratives to acquire sumptuous emotional affect (Kumar 2001). Children—the intended readers—are expected to identify with them so as to develop faith in the causes that drove them as heroes. In the case of India, the hero is Mahatma Gandhi, and in the case of Pakistan, the hero is Jinnah. Their personalities emerge from the texts like giant-size cut-outs, personifying the nations they represent and symbolically gave birth to. The contrast between their personalities and lifestyles serves as a sign pointing to the contrast that the two nations are supposed to signify between the ideologies on which they are based. The exercise is completed by mutual vilification—that of Gandhi in the Pakistani narrative, and of Jinnah in the Indian narrative.

They embody the nation-building project which has elements of jubilation and pride as well as grief and tragedy in each case. The element of pride and celebration in India's case comes from winning against colonial masters and their designs; in Pakistan's case, both pride and joy are associated with birth despite the desperate attempts made to prevent its birth as a nation. The tragedy, in the case of India, is Partition; the tragedy, in the case of Pakistan, is that while Partition represented birth, it did not offer territorial justice.

These contrasting constructions necessarily assume that the two nation states are not just based on different principles, but that their internal worlds, comprising demographic and cultural realities, also differ. We can now turn towards examining this assumption. The Indian narrative, which is not necessarily reflected in all state-level textbooks (Kumar 2017), is designed to represent a nation where the religious life of the population is subservient to their civic life. Secularism as a principle of statecraft is rather different from secularism as a symbolic statement of nationhood. In the context of statecraft, it provides India with a useful means whereby the state can perform its various functions in a demographically and culturally diverse social environment. However, as a symbolic representation of nationhood, secularism has remained an inadequate idiom inasmuch as its validity as a descriptor comes from its denial of the importance and role of religion in shaping everyday life. This is one reason why the term 'secularism' as state ideology has remained subject to interpretation (Kesavan 2001) and has allowed revivalist politics to mobilise support. The instrumentality of 'secularism' as a linguistic tool to distinguish India from Pakistan has proved weak, and with the passage of time, it has been showing signs of failure with increasing frequency.

On India's treatment of secularism as a representation of its nationhood, one can ask: Does India have a choice? In other words, India can hardly be expected to drop the idiom of secularism and thereby accept the colonial assumption that Partition was based on religious lines and its purpose was to separate a Muslim Pakistan from a Hindu India. There were indeed serious problems with this colonial discourse, and its truth value remains very poor. Be that as it may, India's narrative of its own history does not need to deny Hindu religiosity.

The term 'popular Hinduism' is often used to distinguish ritual and myth from abstract or spiritual Hinduism. This distinction is yet another example of the discomfort inherent in the ideological usage of secularism. Secular voices hesitate to accept religiosity as a major aspect of common life, and this hesitation enables the consolidation of revivalist politics which focuses on profiling Hindu-ness.

The crisis that Pakistan has faced is not altogether different. Its adoption of Islam as a nationalist creed has meant the denial of the diverse forms that popular Islam has taken in its population. Once Islam was declared as a marker of the newly formed nation's single, state-authenticised identity, the considerable diversity of practices and beliefs, myth and ritual that characterises popular Islam in Pakistan had to be ignored or suppressed in the official narrative fed to the young in schools.

These developments also led to mutual stereotyping. In Pakistan's official narrative—and the discourse upholding it—India's claim to being a secular country is labelled as humbug. For Pakistan, India is simply Hindu, and Hinduism is a fixed set of practices and beliefs, one being the belief that Islam poses an evil threat to Hinduism. This belief justifies fear and the projection of a common hatred in India towards Muslims and Pakistan. As stereotypes do not allow room for nuances or any kind of differentiation, the Pakistani stereotype of India allows no scope for the thought that Indians may hold diverse views and perceptions.

On the Indian side, the stereotype of Pakistan is that of a country signifying monolithic Islam which allows recognition of no other religion as worthy of faith, certainly not Hinduism. The idea that all Muslims are one and so are Pakistanis, that they are united in their belief that Pakistan need not exist as an independent country, is central to this stereotype. Here too, hatred is a core emotion, to be kept alive as a guide for cautionary, suspicious behaviour towards a geographically unavoidable neighbour. The stereotypes that the two nations maintain serve as frames drawing strength from chosen episodes of history going as far back as required. In India's case, the image of Muslims as an invader and marauder is available in medieval past. In Pakistan, the imaginary of the wily Hindu is available in the freedom struggle, particularly in the resistance shown to the idea of Partition which was necessary for the birth of Pakistan.

Education and Socialisation

This insight needs to be examined with care and conceptual wherewithal, otherwise we will miss the key benefits such a case study of conflict between two nations might offer for developing a general theory of the relation between education and peace. One thing that my study (Kumar 2001; Kumar 2007) of the Indo–Pak case brings out most crisply is that a conflict can be guaranteed to persist and hold its potential for violence if its seeds are sown early in life so as to enter primary socialisation. This term has conceptual value specific to sociology of culture. It tends to get rather limited, and somewhat diluted, attention in the field of education. This is mainly because education is perceived more as a domain of practice and policy than as a field of enquiry, whereas sociology is regarded primarily as a field of enquiry along with other social sciences. Therefore, in education, socialisation is studied mainly to adjust pedagogic effort to the influences the child might carry from home.

The depth at which early socialisation shapes self-identity, attitudes and values is often underestimated by those involved in education, such as teachers and curriculum designers. If we hold early socialisation as a major factor involved in the construction of self-identity and outlook towards those regarded as the 'other', we will be on firm ground if we say that hatred and hostility between nations gains a self-perpetuating momentum when education at school adds to a prejudice already prevailing in the social ethos. To elucidate this role of schooling and curriculum, we will need to examine the complex relations that underpin any process of institutionalised learning in modern society, namely, relations between education and socialisation. These relations are important for the learning involved in any school subject, including those covered in the natural and the social sciences, mathematics and language. The relationship between education at school and socialisation at home plays a key role in shaping the learning of history. Before we embark on our specific enquiry about India and Pakistan, let us discuss briefly why learning about the past or history forms a critical factor in the role of schooling in the context of peace.

The social, unlike the physical, world surrounding a young person cannot be discovered without assistance and encouragement or guidance. Physical objects and happenings, such as the rising of the moon in a darkening sky or a passing train, attract the child and demand attention. Contrastingly, information about how parents got married or about events that happened a long time ago gains a child's attention and a place in his or her consciousness only when pointed out and narrated in one form or another. The young depend on adults for learning about the past. By the time children enrol at school, they have already 'learned' a great deal about the past at home—from the adults who look after them and the resources, such as television, that a modern home possesses. The school waits for several years before starting to teach history; learning about the past at home, on the other hand, starts in infancy itself, and continues as part of routine life at home.

Children's absorption of knowledge about the past takes place at home in its own unique ethos without the interference of reflective thought, questioning or awareness of alternative narratives or explanation. It occurs with substantial emotional content which is characteristic of primary socialisation (Berger and Luckmann 1966). The narrative is not necessarily woven into an integrated story. Rather, it is sporadic, fragmented and interspersed by visual, auditory and other forms of sensory experience. Quasi-historical knowledge, some of which borders on myth, is interwoven with religious beliefs and attitudes including attitudes towards 'others' who have a different history. A sense of community is embedded in this amorphous body of quasi-historical knowledge, and this sense imparts an identity to the small child. It marks separation from others who belong to a different 'community'.

Normally, we do not view children's religious experience as an induction or immersion into history. We feel reluctant, even unwilling, to do so because we are used to classifying history as a documentary field of study based on facts and evidence. We tend to ignore and to denigrate perceptual history (Kumar 2007) which is nourished and sustained by memory of experience spanning several generations. The history inherent in religion is similar. It covers long stretches of time, covering the pre-formation, growth and subsequent development periods of a faith system, with its attendant ideas, beliefs and collectively held memories. Characters or personalities, sometimes held at the level of myth, are a part of this faith system. Its value as a shared or collectively owned memory-record is crucial to the selfhood or identity it imparts to a group. It is so crucial to the group's survival and intellectual well-being that it is passed on to the newly born at the earliest possible moment and the imparting continues throughout infancy and childhood, ensuring deep imprinting in the mind. As imprinting, it is impervious to doubt or question. It serves as a well-ploughed field for the knowledge of history imparted at school in later childhood. This process whereby primary socialisation at home merges into, and is consolidated by, secondary socialisation at school is sharply illustrated in the case of Indo–Pak antipathy maintained over seven decades now. By examining it, we can grasp the difficulties and challenges that education presents for the pursuit of peace between two hostile nations.

Three Models

The past constitutes the most challenging domain of knowledge from the point of view of developing a peace perspective. The role of education at school is critical in this respect. More specifically, the role comprises a choice between two alternatives with reference to the socialisation of the young at home. Education at school can either supplement the socialisation that has occurred at home or, alternatively, the school can differ from home and socialise the child into a new orientation towards the past. To analyse home–school relations, in the context of education for peace, let me refer to a typology I have presented in my book *Battle for Peace*. It offers three models as shown in Figure 2. Model 1 covers educational systems where home and school overlap, implying a marked continuity between socialisation at home and formal learning at school. Model 2 presents the opposite case where home and school are detached and indifferent to each other.

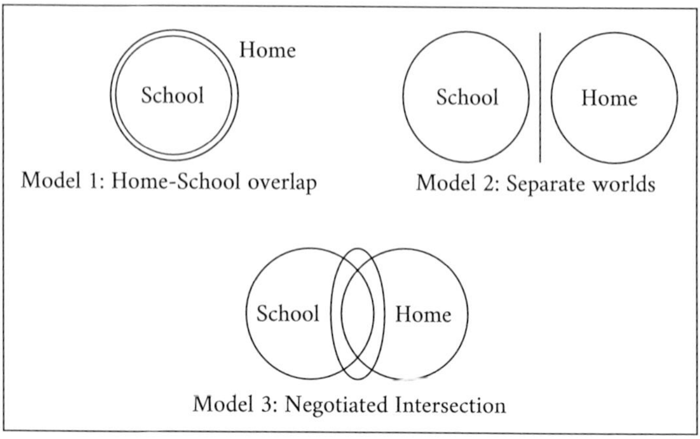

Figure 2: Three models of the home–school relationship (Kumar 2007, 199).

Model 3 offers the possibility of interaction and negotiation between the two.

These models help us to capture the complex relationship between schooling and learning through socialisation at home in India and Pakistan. Both countries inherit colonial policies in education which enable schooling to stay aloof from home culture (Kumar 2014). Since Independence, the two countries have pursued divergent paths in the matter of religious instruction at school. It is an essential part of the daily school routine in Pakistan, whereas in India it is prohibited, except in minority schools (UNESCO MGIEP 2017). Thus, educational policy in Pakistan adheres to Model 1 while in India it adheres to Model 2. The pursuit of Islamisation in Pakistani policy over the recent decades has further sharpened the use of school education for promoting a nationalistic perspective based on religion and the distinction with regard to India on the basis of religious difference.

In India, the policy scenario presents a more complex and somewhat volatile picture. Curricular reforms undertaken on the basis of the National Curriculum Framework (NCF) 2005 (NCERT 2006) point towards an attempt to apply Model 3. Under this model, the school tries to engage with the child's life at home. This goal is reflected in the National Council of Educational Research and Training (NCERT) textbooks based on NCF. Schools administered under the norms of the Central Board of Secondary Education (CBSE) are obliged to use NCERT textbooks. These schools constitute less than ten per cent of the total number of secondary schools in the country. Other schools follow state-level syllabi and textbooks. In many states, the recent years have witnessed the rise of religious nationalism as a political ideology. It has impacted textbooks and the school ethos in several states. The attempt made in NCF 2005 to promote a secular perspective and peace-oriented values has not proved easy to pursue in the states. This attempt followed a two-pronged approach: one, to redesign syllabi and textbooks so as to provide room for critical reflection on culture and history; and two, to prioritise peace values such as tolerance, non-violence and conflict resolution through negotiation. Although no major review has taken place with regard to the implementation of NCF, its general impact on India's vast and complex system is undeniable. How far it will be sustained remains to be seen.

Citizen and the Nation

History is not the only subject nurturing collective antagonisms during childhood. Its role is supplemented by the early introduction of political boundaries and civic responsibilities. The school curriculum is mostly out of step with children's cognitive development in geography and civics. Well before children can grasp the mathematical and geometrical concepts involved in the preparation of maps, they are exposed to maps showing the territorial boundaries of the nation. Identification with the territorial nation proceeds parallel to the teaching in yet another area of knowledge out of step with children's intellectual development. This is knowledge about the state and the functions of the government.

In many countries, this latter knowledge articulately demands loyalty to the nation state and willingness to sacrifice one's life as a test of this loyalty. This aspect of the civics curriculum has gone through radical changes in India under recent curricular reforms through which civics has been renamed 'Social and Political Life'. This new subject attempts to use children's own curiosity about how the social world is formed and how some of the older social divisions are challenged by humanistic assertions of a political nature (Gupta 2015). Though this new construction of knowledge has not spread to all regions of India, it is a marked departure from the older teaching of civics which continues to dominate the social studies curriculum in Pakistan. Indeed, social studies there is subsumed under the subject called 'Pakistan Studies', which is directly aimed at cultivating unflinching commitment to a militaristic, masculine state (Saigol 2015).

Nationalism and children's education are firmly welded together in all parts of the world. The use of school education for propaganda has a long history of its own, and the history demonstrates a strong affinity with the rise of identity-driven political ideologies. These ideologies have found fertile ground in the current political and economic climate prevailing in many countries in different parts of the world (*The Economist* 2017). In Asia, a recent study of curriculum policies of twenty-two countries found the promotion of national identity as the most frequently mentioned aim of education (UNESCO MGIEP 2017).

Regimentation

When the promotion of a strong nationalistic feeling is actively defined as the aim of education from the earliest stage, it exacerbates the phenomenon of regimentation in schools. Regimentation has been closely associated with mass education in every region of the world. Many regard it as an essential aspect of education, and go to the extent of accepting it as a process that creates the enabling conditions for teaching. Indeed, this view is so common and popular that a plea for making education more child-centric and less regimenting is dismissed as being unrealistic and therefore pointless. Old concepts of learning demanded the child's undirected energy to be brought under control, and the harshest means for achieving this goal were considered legitimate. The teacher's right to inflict corporal punishment of any kind was an important aspect of his authority. School and classroom rituals of various kinds were used to create a culture of compliance. These have become part and parcel of school routines to such an extent that they are often treated as signifiers of quality and rigour. Terms like 'good discipline' are used to praise the efficacy of a school in subduing any expression of individuality by children, except through officially approved channels.

The term 'discipline' is often used to refer to a certain kind of moral education. In his attempt to analyse ideas about discipline and moral education, Clark (1998) found that traditional ideas are incoherent and unworkable, yet they remain dominant. Enforcement of school uniform, hairstyle and shoes, slogan shouting and militaristic drills and marching are common features of what is considered a well-functioning school. Together, they enable school authorities to construct concrete, visual evidence of efficiency and order. They serve as elements of a habitus that acquires self-perpetuating or autonomous power over children. Its symbolic power has been recognised as a form of violence by researchers in different educational systems, following Bourdieu's theorisation of habitus (Bourdieu 1991). In a study of school culture, Yadav (2014) identified several aspects of regimentation in the daily ritual of morning assembly. Collective slogan shouting, marching to martial tunes and collective listening to the principal's messages were among the routines included in the morning assembly. It enabled schools to achieve an ethos where children's individual personalities could submerge into an orchestrated whole. The use of school uniforms to merge individual identities is common across many countries. Horvat and Antonio (1999) have examined how these means of control affect the lives of Afro-American girls.

Evaluation is yet another aspect of schooling that has provided a fertile site for regimentation to deepen and grow. Classroom tests and annual examinations are an integral part of contemporary school culture. They are used not merely to motivate children to work hard but also to promote competition among them. This latter aspect has gained prominence partly because it resonates the wider ethos of market-centred policies in every sphere of life. Attempts to encourage child-centred methods of teaching have failed to soften the hold of exams on teachers, parents and children. Opposition to progressive curricular reforms is articulated by referring to the utility of tests and exams for instilling fear of losing out and encouraging discipline. The emotional value invested in exam success finds strong consensus between teachers and parents. Starting at the earliest stage of schooling, the regime of tests and exams reinforces the terror that schools cultivate. A recent upsurge of 'outcome-driven' policies have reinforced testing and exam routines in schools. In the Right to Education (RTE) Act passed by the Indian parliament in 2009, the practice of annual exams that divide children into 'pass' and 'fail' categories was replaced by a Continuous and Comprehensive Evaluation (CCE) process. This shift has been under assault and the demand for reverting to the old exam system has been getting louder.

Learning at school is permeated by a continuously reinforced fear of consequences of diverse kinds, including that of failing in an exam. In an essay on her own encounter with primary schooling, Kadyan (2008) describes the general regime of fear that a small child's mind internalises. She says:

> Many parts of my school I had heard of but never seen and I am sure that there must have been others which I had not even heard of. How could I risk my life simply to know the school building fully, when every time one tried, one faced the highest probability of meeting a heartless devil given charge of keeping children inside their allotted cells? The only thing that belonged to me was my seat. I hated all the occasions that required me to move from it. Who knows when someone might snatch that seat away from me, accusing me of being a bad learner?

Kadyan's autobiographical narrative brings out the impact that the school ethos has on a child's mind by alienating them and exercising total physical control. The numbing of children's intellect is achieved by schools at an early stage, not necessarily deliberately or as a project although that too may be the case under certain circumstances. A great deal of regimentation of the body is built into the school's daily routine. It covers things like walking, standing and sitting, but more significantly it covers how they will talk, respond to a question asked, or raise a question or point if such a behaviour is permitted at all. Even as this discussion echoes Foucault's architecture of terror, it must be supplemented by a reference to the pedagogic routines that occupy children's time with inconsequential, repetitive exercise of power. These have been described by LaDousa (2015) in his ethnographic study of the languages of schooling in Varanasi. Some of the routines he describes are part of a 'time pass' strategy which conditions learners into accepting the school as a space where endurance of triviality and meaninglessness is the key to survival and progress.

The Counterargument

A great deal of critical commentary made during the 1960s and the 1970s in the US, UK and some other countries brought to light the depth to which school-induced numbing of children's intellectual capacities can go. Holt's *How Children Fail* (1964) is a classic of that period. Other works, such as Kozol's *Death at an Early Age* (1968), remind us that the numbing process may include a political function—that of maintaining inherited structures of social and economic dominance through the pervasive marginalisation of the poor. Regimentation as a tool of subduing children's intellectual agency figures well before the 1960s as a subject of philosophical interest. The plea for 'child-centred' methods has a political edge in the progressive writers, pedagogues and thinkers of the inter-war years. Among them, Maria Montessori, Bertrand Russell and Sri Aurobindo wrote eloquently about the role that collective controlling of the minds of the young plays in school in making them vulnerable as adults to political propaganda, especially that of state-managed nationalistic propaganda. They cautioned against the collective ego represented by the state as it tends to suppress the creative energies available for shaping the future. Rabindranath Tagore too criticised political nationalism as it discourages humanistic values and ideals. His short story, 'The Parrot's Tale', captures the tragedy whereby the natural instincts and capacities of the child are shown to be in contest with the brute power of the state, and the child loses. Recent additions to this lineage of thinkers are J. Krishnamurti, Paulo Freire and Ivan Illich. They were iconoclastic and positive about the possibility of a radical restructuring of public learning. Their critique of prevailing education was harsh, and it reminds us that educational reform cannot occur in isolation from change in other institutions of society, including the state.

In our attempt to look for philosophical guidance to develop both a critique of education and a means to reform it, we can find in Gandhi's experiments in politics and education a creative answer. His life as a pacifist political thinker and his legacy of non-violent struggle against oppressive imperial rule make him a major figure in the history of ideas (Parel 2016). Throughout his life he remained eager to seek an educational means for breaking the cycle of economic oppression and violence. His proposal for the use of traditional crafts as a means to reconstruct education is often seen in purely economic terms, that is, as a route to changing attitudes to manual work and cultivating self-reliance. This conventional reading of Gandhi's 'nai talim' (new education) has been critiqued in two recent investigations (Gaur 2016; Srinivasan 2019). These scholars have made independent attempts to reconstruct Gandhi's epistemology from the wider corpus of his ideas and engagements. For Srinivasan, Gandhi's view of knowledge should be defined in the context of a theory of ethical learning which responds to the problems of human social existence in the widest possible sense. Gaur locates the centre of his pedagogic plan in the concept of Swaraj or self-rule wherein he offers a means to define human freedom. Gaur has used the concept of Swaraj to study Anand Niketan, a school started by Gandhi which has recently been revived. It serves children from villages located in the vicinity of Gandhi's ashram at Sevagram. Children's lives and activities, especially those related to environment education and craft work, offer considerable evidence to say that Gandhi's pedagogic theory encourages self-driven learning.

Similar evidence and direction can be found in the work of Devi Prasad, an art teacher, artist and a world-renowned pacifist.

His experience of teaching art to children at schools started by Tagore and Gandhi enabled him to formulate a full-fledged argument explaining the nature and logic of aesthetic discipline (Prasad 1998). It recognises freedom as the aim of artwork in childhood. Prasad's analytical account of his experience as a teacher establishes how the pursuit of freedom enables children to develop self-awareness, balance, proportion and symmetry, and predisposes them towards peace. Gandhi's political thought also offers us a wider vision for reorganising school subjects such as history and civics. The contribution they make, in their present form, to reinforcing nationalist antagonisms, needs to be critiqued from Gandhi's perspective on modern civilisation and its propensity to encourage fear and aggression.

Contemporary Landscape

The lineage of child-centred ideas and practices in education discussed earlier provides us with the elements of peace education. These are: recognition of the child's agency, and the teacher's role in encouraging children to reflect on their own experience. If we use these basic principles to examine prevailing trends, we find that practices challenged earlier and replaced by child-centred approaches are witnessing a resurgence. The force of this trend is strong and pervasive enough to put any criticism of regimentation on the defensive, lest it be charged of sheer romanticism.

Advances in the technology of communication have served to strengthen instrumentalist ideas in education, both at the level of policy-making and the everyday world of school teaching. The 'new technological environment' described by Elkind (2003) places the child at a receiving end—exposed to forces that parents and teachers cannot fully grasp or deal with. Neo-behaviourist advocacy of scripted curriculum and pedagogy has diminished the teacher's autonomy. These developments are being led by managerial experts who regard education as yet another area where they can bring efficiency. Their intervention has resulted in further erosion of the democratic space available for shaping education as a social institution. The emerging pedagogic landscape is dominated by the use of testing as a means to enhance competitiveness and accountability.

Policy packages echoing the human capital theory justify mechanistic models of learning and teaching. In this scenario, peace education figures as an instrument to be used for tangible purposes. One is to limit the concept of peace itself to a set of behaviours capable of being manipulated and measured. To complete this picture, we must turn towards the economic policy scenario in which recent shifts in education are situated. The term 'neo-liberal' is often used to describe these policies, conveying the tilt towards privatisation in all spheres of social policy, including education. A great deal of scholarship exists on the impact of neo-liberalism on state spending. Research shows a radical increase in expenditure worldwide on armaments, indicating a link between neo-liberalism and militarism (Cypher 2007). This economic trend suggests why nationalism as an ideology is witnessing a revival. After a brief spell of popularity, the discourse of globalisation is already in recession. National interests are serving as the axis of political mobilisation for conservative leadership.

In India, nationalism defined on religio-cultural lines has come into dominance, marginalising older claims to a secular national identity. Erosion of secularism and the propagation of religious separatism through public media and educational institutions has made several regions of northern India look similar to Pakistan, where religion has been the official marker of national identity. In Rajasthan, school textbooks produced by the state government have been revised with a view to promoting among children a politically constructed regional identity based on a distortion of medieval struggles. The new history attempts to use religious identities of medieval warriors to justify a majoritarian national identity for contemporary India. This is not an isolated example of provincial curriculum and textbooks being used for promoting sectarian politics. The gap in Indian curricular planning at federal and provincial levels has been quite pronounced, both in terms of quality and aims. When we consider that provincial textbooks are used in schools serving economically weaker sections of society, we realise how socio-economic inequality adds to the complexity of curricular reform.

Conclusion

Let us conclude by placing the India–Pakistan example discussed earlier in the context of current economic policy scenario. The role education plays in maintaining long-term hostility is unlikely to change without radical reformulation of the aims of education and changes in its content and methods. For such a change to occur, peace education offers a means to question prevailing policies and preferences. It also provides a site for critiquing education itself. Before education can be used to promote peace, its own humanistic potential will have to be rescued. Peace education can be viewed as a site of resistance to the all-round attempt currently underway to push education into becoming a means of total regimentation. In order to make peace education a resistant force, its key elements need to be articulated. One is to restore personal meaning in learning; two, centrality of critical enquiry in any process of institutionalised education; three, importance of justice for making peace sustainable.

These core elements and the interplay among them can be used to seek a direction for reform in education. A major sign of crisis in education is its inability to impart meaning to the experience of attending school or college. As a social institution managed by the state, the school has now become a universally enforced experience of childhood. Though its lure and the legitimacy of schooling have grown enormously, the school's ability to educate has diminished along with its autonomous status and ability to uphold the values constitutive of education as a concept (Miri 2014). Historical changes in the economic and political demands on education have affected its capacity to serve the young in their search for meaning through the exercise of curiosity and enquiry. Affirmation of faith in the potential of education to impart the means to make sense of the world is necessary as a first step towards reforming schools. The idea of global citizenship education can provide some valuable energy and direction in this regard, provided that this idea does not become a matter of advocacy for mechanically made insertions in the curriculum. Education imbued by critical enquiry implies learning to situate oneself where we are in history in order to understand how we got 'here', and thereby to act upon the problems facing us today.

In the study of a conflict, critical enquiry helps us to acknowledge and thereby release the emotive energies buried below the surface behaviour. When the past, which is buried in a conflict, is excavated through enquiry, it allows us to assess the kind and scale of justice required to achieve peace by addressing a conflict. This is crucial for the future to be qualitatively different from the past and present. Education will acquire a transformative role when learners gain from it an experience of enquiry into the sedimented past. They will develop what Yash Pal (2006) called 'a taste of understanding'. It will make 'the present of our children wholesome, creative and enjoyable'.

Defined in this manner, reform in education to make it child-centred necessarily means loosening its power of regimentation. As discussed, this power has multiple sources and it resides in the everyday culture of schooling. But apart from the regimentation embedded in the schooling process itself, a matching imperative comes from the state which imposes on the school the duty to propagate nationalist ideals and imagination. Thus, the school becomes an instrument in the hands of the state to consolidate the civic loyalty of the younger generation in its formative years. This process pushes the school to sacrifice humanistic ideals of education and commit itself to nurturing the committed citizen. The apprehension that the state will use education to prioritise citizens' loyalty over their humanity was recognised by Rousseau (Soetard 1994). His query, whether we can nurture the citizen without injuring the human, has acquired poignant relevance in our times. In numerous cases of hostility between nation states, education nourishes the historically inherited consciousness of hostility more explicitly than it creates the capacity to reconcile with the past (Frieberg and Chung 2017; Kumar 2003). The recovery of humanist ideals and values through education is possible through reconstruction of education itself, aimed at bridging the gap between the concept and the system of education.

References

Berger, Peter, and Thomas Luckmann. 1966. *The Social Construction of Reality*. New York: Anchor Books.

Bourdieu, Pierre. 1991. *Language and Symbolic Power*. Edited by John B. Thompson. Translated by Gino Raymond and Matthew Adamson. Cambridge: Polity.

Bruner, Jerome. 1987. *Actual Minds, Possible Worlds*. Cambridge, Massachusetts: Harvard University Press.

Clark, Charles. 1998. 'Discipline in Schools.' *British Journal of Educational Studies* 46(3): 289–301.

Cohn, Bernard S. 1987. *An Anthropologist among the Historians and Other Essays*. Delhi: Oxford.

Cypher, James M. 2007. 'From Military Keynesianism to Global-Neoliberal Militarism.' *Monthly Review* 59 (2): 37.

Elkind, David. 2003. 'Technology's Impact on Child Growth and Development.' *CIO.com*. https://www.cio.com/article/2441936/david-elkind--technology-s-impact-on-child-growth-and-development.html.

Frieberg, Annika, and C. K. Martin Chung, eds. 2017. *Reconciling with the Past: Resources and Obstacles in a Global Perspective*. London: Routledge.

Gaur, Nidhi. 2016. 'Learning through Crafts: A Study of An Experimental School.' *Vidyapith* 4: 67–82.

Gupta, Latika. 2008. 'Growing up Hindu and Muslim: How Early Does it Happen?' *Economic and Political Weekly* 43:6, 35–41.

——. 2015. 'Making Reflective Citizens: India's New Textbooks for Social and Political Life.' In *Constructing Modern Asian Citizenship*, edited by Edward Vickers and Krishna Kumar, 105–24. London: Routledge.

Holt, John. 1964. *How Children Fail*. New York: Pitman Publishing Corporation.

Horvat, Erin McNamara, and Anthony Lising Antonio. 1999. '"Hey, Those Shoes are out of Uniform": African American Girls in an Elite High School and the Importance of Habitus.' *Anthropology and Education Quarterly*. 30:3, 317. http://www.jstor.org/stable/3196024.

Kadyan, Sonia. 2008. 'My Learning.' *Seminar* 592. https://www.india-seminar.com/2008/592/592_sonia_kadyan.htm

Kakar, Sudhir. 1996. *The Colors of Violence*. Chicago: University of Chicago Press.

Kesavan, Mukul. 2001. *Secular Common Sense*. New Delhi: Penguin.

Kozol, Jonathan. 1968. *Death at an Early Age*. New York: Barnes and Noble.

Kumar, Krishna. 2001. *Prejudice and Pride: School Histories of the Freedom Struggle in India and Pakistan*. New Delhi: Viking.

——. 2003. 'Peace with the Past.' *India Seminar* 522. http://www.india-seminar.com/2003/522/522%20krishna%20kumar.htm.

——. 2007. *Battle for Peace*. New Delhi: Penguin.

——. 2016. *Education, Conflict and Peace*. New Delhi: Orient BlackSwan.

Kumar, Krishna, and Joachim Oesterheld, eds. 2006. *Social Change and Education in South Asia*. New Delhi: Orient BlackSwan.

LaDousa, Chaise. 2015. *Hindi is our Ground, English is our Sky*. Cambridge: Cambridge University Press.

Miri, Mrinal. 2014. *Philosophy and Education*. New Delhi: Oxford University Press.

NCERT. 2006. *National Curriculum Framework 2005*. New Delhi: NCERT.

Pal, Yash. 2006. 'Foreword.' In *National Curriculum Framework 2005*. New Delhi: NCERT.

Parel, Anthony J. 2016. *Pax Gandhiana: The Political Philosophy of Mahatma Gandhi*. Oxford: Oxford University Press.

Prasad, Devi. 1998. *Art, the Basis of Education*. New Delhi: National Book Trust.

Razzack, Azra. 1991. 'Growing up Muslim.' *India Seminar*, 387, November: 30–33.

Saigol, Rubina. 2015. 'The Making of the Pakistani Citizen: Civics Education and State Nationalism in Pakistan.' In *Constructing Modern Asian Citizenship*, edited by Edward Vickers and Krishna Kumar, 175–95. London: Routledge.

Sinha, D. ed. 1984. *Socialization of the Indian Child*. New Delhi: Concept.

Soetard, Michel. 1994. 'Jean-Jacques Rousseau.' *Prospects* 24, 3/4: 423–37.

Srinivasan, Shashikala. 2019. *Liberal Education and its Discontents*. New Delhi: Routledge.

The Economist. 2017. 'Whither Nationalism?' *The Economist*. https://www.economist.com/christmas-specials/2017/12/19/whither-nationalism.

UNESCO MGIEP. 2017. *Rethinking Schooling for the 21st Century: The State of Education for Peace, Sustainable Development and Global Citizenship in Asia*. New Delhi: UNESCO MGIEP.

Yadav, P. 2014. 'Vidyalaya ki sanskriti: ek adhyayan.' (Unpublished M.Ed. dissertation, University of Delhi).

6

Equality under a Post-Welfare State

This paper is based on a Malcolm Adiseshiah Memorial lecture delivered at the Madras Institute of Development Studies in 2017.

With the promulgation of the Right to Education (RTE) Act in 2009, the long-cherished policy goal of universalisation of elementary schooling seemed to have come within the nation's reach. Scholarly advocacy of universal access to elementary education (for example, Naik 1975) had assumed that when schools can enrol and retain all children, this would enhance educational equality. Universality, however, does not necessarily mean equality. Why that is so can be examined both in terms of factors external to the system of education and also in terms of impediments embedded in the system of education itself. This paper first probes the latter kind of impediments. Specifically, it analyses the structurally maintained relations between primary, secondary and higher education. Regarded as different stages of education through which a young person passes, terms like 'primary', 'secondary' and 'higher' are commonly perceived as distinct components of the system. Routine common sense guides the popular view that the quality of higher education depends on the quality of primary and secondary education. Relations between the three segments of the system are seldom examined as such. This paper will attempt to demonstrate how the relations between primary, secondary and higher education constitute a set of impediments that do not allow universal schooling to enhance equality. For undertaking this analysis, the paper looks into the text of the RTE Act and the critique it carries of the prevailing system of elementary education. For examining the interaction between school and higher education, the paper will focus on teacher training as an overlapping sector. It will also take into account the impact made on school and teacher-training policies by the growing presence and scope of a technology-centric market of pedagogic goods. Subsequent to this analysis of systemic impediments, external obstacles entrenched in the nature of the post-welfare state and its expectations from education will be examined.

Historical Background

Starting with the latter half of the nineteenth century, universalisation of initial schooling gradually spread to all corners of the world. This phenomenon can be described as a movement which has influenced the meaning of the term 'education' and its variants in different languages. The movement is still unfolding and spreading. It has reached South Asia only recently, and in India it continues to be a subject of debate on the roles of state and society (Mehendale 2018). Debates of this kind have raged in other parts of the world earlier. They are intertwined with economic, political and legal matters, and in many cases, with cultural issues as well. The question of responsibility has been quite central to these debates, mainly in the financial sphere, because the attempt to universalise schooling, even for a few years, costs vast sums of money. Should it be paid by the state or by the family, that is, the parents of a child? This kind of question typically entails the assumption, and the belief underlying it, that school education is beneficial for society as a whole and also for the child who receives it. These benefits cannot be defined and listed without referring to what we might call the demands of modernity, more specifically, the needs that arise when an economy goes through 'modernisation'—a term associated with a state-led attempt to encourage the growth of a modern, industrial economy. Modernity as the goal to be reached through the process of modernisation is widely viewed as being associated with universal literacy and democracy.

It is assumed that modernisation calls for a literate citizenry. Thus, the citizen who works in an industrial economy also forms a unit of the political order assumed to be upholding the modern kind of economy. This desired political order is customarily labelled as 'democracy', which is said to be dependent on universal literacy. This labelling is inadequate and also somewhat misleading. Democracy and industrial economy are not necessarily related as many societies have registered industrial growth without witnessing the growth of basic values and provisions of a democratic order (Moore 1968). 'Modernity' too remains a problematic term, especially with reference to modernisation, which has been pursued in many parts of the world under conditions that do not conform to any clear definition of democracy (Touraine 1998).

Some historical references may be useful at this point. The movement towards universalisation of initial, or what is often called, basic school education in England was quite slow to unfold and progress. For children to attend schools, they had to be freed from the responsibility of working to contribute to the family income. Child labour took a long time to be effectively outlawed, partly because of socio-economic constraints, but also because of political reasons. Consensus was not easy to achieve despite a functioning system of debate in legislative forums, not just because of entrenched attitudes, but also because the propertied and entrepreneurial strata held vested interest in the availability of cheap child labour. The struggle to legislate and support universal basic education in England went on until the early twentieth century, and the parallel struggle to democratise basic school education, in the sense of ensuring equitable quality in inequal social settings, continued till after the end of the Second World War in the mid-twentieth century (Lawson and Silver 1973).

In contrast to this prolonged and sluggish movement, Japan made radical and speedy progress towards universal schooling under the Meiji rulers. Under conditions sharply different from those of England (Kobayashi 1976), both politically and economically, Japan achieved near-universal schooling for its children by compelling the peasantry to release children from the farm. Japan's story may sound somewhat unique and exotic as its struggles for democracy and universal schooling remained quite separate. However, it shares some similarities with the enforcement of schooling on children and literacy on adults witnessed in different parts of the twentieth century under communist states in societies as different as those of Russia and China, Cuba and Vietnam. These experiences, and others from some countries of mainland western Europe, remind us that the relation between universal school education and industrialisation of the economy is far from sequential. In many cases, like that of the Scandinavian countries, the spread of schooling followed rather than preceded industrial growth and the development of a modern state—not necessarily democratic in every case. This indeterminacy continues to be seen at the regional level in countries that have achieved high rates of growth in their industrial economy or are attempting to attain it now.

These historical lessons are highly relevant, even instructive, for India, where an industrial economy is in a nascent state and, on account of several different factors, is struggling to spread and grow against the resistance of 'rurality', a term I will use to cover an agrarian system of livelihood as well as a specific kind of cultural ethos (Kumar 2013). The Indian story of universal schooling has just begun in the early twenty-first century. It formally started with the passage of the RTE Act through the parliament in 2009. The background of this important legal enactment is long, complex and patchy. The RTE has come into force as a result of the amendment made in 2002 in the Constitution. Originally, the Constitution had no specific mention of an educational right. What it offered was Article 45 in Part IV which lists the 'directive principles of state policy'. Article 45 offered one such principle, directing the state to provide free and compulsory education to all children aged six to fourteen. Under this provision, the Constitution recognised universal schooling as a moral responsibility of the state, not a justiciable right that could be claimed by citizens. The right now known as RTE elaborates on the amendment made to Article 21, which occurs in Part III of the Constitution, where fundamental and justiciable rights of the citizen are listed. Article 21 covers the citizen's right to life. It has now been amended through the insertion of an additional clause which reads as follows: 'The State shall provide free and compulsory education to all children of the age of six to fourteen years in such manner as the State may, by law, determine'. Before this clause was added, Article 21 offered a right to life. Through legal intervention and conceptual elaboration over several years, Article 21 acquired the capacity to offer the right to a life of dignity. RTE concretises this aspect of a citizen's life. For this reason, we can say RTE treats education as a resource of dignity in an individual's life. It describes the measures that the state is legally bound to pursue in order to ensure universal access to eight years of compulsory school education during childhood.

Education, Dignity and Equality

The school is where the citizenry will access this element of dignity during childhood. Given this legal background, RTE presents education as something more than entry into a school at the age of six. The eight years covered by RTE are supposed to provide an experience of learning that would make future life worthwhile in the sense of carrying the prospect of being led with dignity. How precisely educational experience might impart this particular trait to the future life of a citizen is indicated quite amply in the various sections of RTE. These indications comprise what one might call an agenda or policy of educational reform, and in this sense, RTE offers more than a mere right. It also indicates how that right is to be delivered.

This special quality of RTE can be seen as a response to the problem that any right granted to children would face—namely, the problem of children's dependence on their adult guardians to ensure the delivery of the right. This dependence arises from the natural fact that children cannot claim a right on their own. RTE indicates some of the means by which the right to be at a school for eight years is to be experienced. It suggests the measures that must be taken for creating the enabling conditions and the institutional wherewithal necessary for implementation. Moreover, many of the clauses where these indications are given can be read as criticism of the prevailing system of education.

Let us look at some of these clauses. We can divide them into two broad categories. In the first category, we can include the norms to be followed by the system. Pupil-teacher ratio, the grades under RTE, teacher's involvement in work other than teaching and the deployment of teachers are covered. All of these emanate from RTE's implicit critique of the system. For instance, the age span covered by RTE is expressed in terms of two distinct stages, 'primary' and 'upper-primary', which together constitute an eight-year span of 'elementary' education. The primary stage comprises the first five years and the upper-primary stage the remaining three years. RTE's enunciation of these divisions has already begun to reshape and streamline initial schooling in many of the Indian states which were following a seven-year cycle, divided into four years of primary and three years of upper-primary stages. In certain states, the curriculum for the upper-primary stage is prepared by the secondary board. This practice will have to be changed in order to attain conformity with RTE's terminology that places primary and upper-primary stages under a composite 'elementary' stage.

Similarly, the mandated overall ratio of thirty children per teacher for the elementary stage as a whole conveys a critique of large classes managed by less than the required number of teachers, which is a common situation in many parts of India. RTE goes further and specifies that schools must have subject-wise teachers at the upper-primary stage. The schedule given in RTE also asks for part-time teachers to be available in every school for the teaching of arts and crafts and physical education. To reinforce its vision of pedagogic norms and standards, RTE summarily prohibits corporal punishment, which is a common practice in Indian schools of all different kinds. Equally significantly, RTE bans annual examinations taken by a board. At present, many states conduct a board examination at the end of Class V and Class VIII. And in certain states, an annual centralised examination is taken every year, starting with Class I. These examinations categorise children into 'pass' and 'fail', requiring those who 'fail' to repeat a grade. In place of annual examination, RTE mandates the implementation of a Continuous and Comprehensive Evaluation (CCE) system, which requires an ongoing assessment of all the different aspects of a child's academic progress and growth.

In the second category we can place RTE's listing of pedagogic practices to be followed by teachers. Under Section V, as many as five clauses list the practices required for imparting elementary education of good quality. These are child-centred pedagogic practices involving activities and experiences that contribute to children's all-round development. CCE, which has been mentioned earlier, is part of this list. The most important aspect of Section V is the instruction that no discrimination is practised in the classroom on the basis of caste, class or gender. This instruction constitutes an explicit critique and disapproval of a common reality portrayed in many studies of school education in India (for example, Nambissan 2009). By summarily prohibiting discriminatory pedagogic behaviour, RTE puts a major responsibility on the state, and anyone else providing elementary education, to create and maintain an egalitarian ethos in the classroom.

The concern for equality is conveyed most sharply in another clause where RTE provides for twenty-five per cent reservation of seats in privately run fee-charging schools for children belonging to the 'economically weaker sections' (EWS) of society. This radical provision is not specifically aimed at universal enrolment, nor does it presume that elementary education of equitable quality will become accessible to all children if the private sector of schools makes its contribution. RTE's aims are higher, in the sense that it conveys a moral agenda for Indian society and state. RTE attempts to cover a complex set of factors that constitute the enabling conditions for its own success. As mentioned earlier, RTE responds to the amended Constitution's call (that is, by the eighty-sixth amendment, covering article 21) for re-equipping the right to life so that the life it protects is capable of being lived with dignity. The various provisions RTE makes for ensuring an active and positive school experience for children—all children, including those whose backgrounds or gender make them vulnerable to discrimination and exclusion—can be described as ingredients of humanistic and socially transformative education. This is why we can say that RTE belongs, conceptually, to the welfarist idea of the state which imparts to state authority a strong agency to interfere with social reality, comprising—and sustained with the help of—traditions and other cultural constructs. This is quite different from the notion of an enabler state that merely serves a limited role of governance, expecting and allowing the market to work and grow.

RTE's Legacy and Initial Experience

RTE's own historical legacy contrasts with the historical moment in which it became an object of legislation. The legacy it represents spans India's struggle to acquire independent nationhood by engaging with the colonial state. In embryonic form, RTE first appeared in 1911 in the imperial Legislative Assembly when Gopal Krishna Gokhale introduced a bill to make primary education compulsory and free. Given the conditions of the time, the bill intended to cover only boys. For girls, early marriage and motherhood were the norm, and the first child-marriage prevention law was eighteen years away. But even for boys, Gokhale's bill offered a bold, radical protection from serving as child labour in the farms owned by powerful land owners. One such person, the Raja of Darbhanga (Bihar), who was a member of the Legislative Assembly, strongly opposed Gokhale's bill by asking in a pointed manner who might work in his fields and maintain agricultural production if all boys below the age of eleven were compelled to attend schools.

This perspective continued to provide the basis for opposition to ban child labour in a summary, rather than in a selective, manner. The incomplete legal triangle—formed by laws attempting to prevent child marriage, others attempting to address child labour, and the state laws to provide for free primary education—ensured that children's access to school education remained a reluctantly recognised responsibility of the state. In the late twentieth century, Weiner (1984) noted the deep-set attitudes of the educated middle class in his attempt to explain the state's reluctance to make access to primary education universal. The political discourse always preferred a financial explanation which was reflected in the term 'the state's capacity', used frequently during the drafting of the Constitution. In Article 45 (that is, before the eighty-sixth amendment), the Constitution offered what Naik (1975) called a 'promise' to India's children. Naik's advocacy of universalisation of elementary education was based on the assumption that the state needed a workable plan to overcome its hesitation to fulfil a moral responsibility which it had accepted despite the knowledge that it was beyond its financial and administrative capacity to fulfil.

When RTE was enacted and promulgated, it seemed as if the state's financial capacity had caught up with the demand that the task of universalising elementary education makes upon the public exchequer. This impression was grounded in the results that the national flagship programme Sarva Shiksha Abhiyan (SSA) had achieved. Like its predecessor, namely the District Primary Education Programme (DPEP), SSA was driven by a generous fund flow from the centre to the states, while the centre's own resources were enhanced by contributions from international donor agencies. During its first five years (2002–07), SSA created an ethos of plentiful financial resources that enabled many new ideas to germinate in the system of elementary education. These included the provision of teacher-support systems at the sub-district level, rapid construction of school buildings, supply of pedagogic resources to teachers, etc. Enrolment and retention both increased at an impressive pace and universal access came within the reach of an institutional apparatus that had earlier struggled with chronically high dropout rates, especially in the populous states of northern India.

However, the sense of plenty that SSA had created did not last long after RTE's promulgation. The centre's largesse represented financial support in a project mode that bypassed the old systemic structures such as the Directorate of Education. Direct funding from the centre under a project mode served the immediate goal of increasing enrolment and retention. It created the expectation that states would pursue systemic reform and maintain increased funding for elementary education from their own resources after the completion of SSA as a project. To an extent, the southern states were able to maintain increased financial resources, though without comprehensive systemic reforms, but the northern states started showing signs of very poor capacity. Within a short while after the promulgation of RTE, SSA started to look like a pleasant memory. As a law, RTE began to lose steam, especially on aspects of systemic and pedagogic practices that it intended to change.

Opponents of different provisions made in the RTE Act approached the courts. One of the first aspects to come under attack was the provision of reservation of twenty-five per cent seats for EWS children. This attack did not attain success. The Supreme Court upheld the provision, but agreed to exempt unaided boarding schools and those run by religious and linguistic minorities. Next came the assault on RTE's attempt to prohibit annual examinations and the pass–fail system. Many state governments, and even the Central Ministry of Human Resource Development (as the Ministry of Education was called back then), were keen to re-establish the annual exam system. A committee appointed by the Central Advisory Board of Education (CABE) recommended that states should be left free to decide on the mode of evaluation. Now that the amendment has been made and many states have started implementing it, the larger agenda of RTE to reform the system stands impaired.

Resistance to RTE

By now it is clear that RTE has been interpreted mainly as an instrument of universality by improving access. Its capacity to equalise the quality of educational experience is facing resistance. Within less than a decade of its promulgation, it has met with serious obstacles that specifically hit its egalitarian potential. These obstacles are of different kinds: some are within the system of education itself while others are in the wider framework and ethos of state policy. We will discuss the obstacles to RTE in four categories. The first is within the system of school education, the second in the relation between school and higher education, the third systemic obstacle is in teacher training and the fourth is in the economic and social policy framework of the post-welfare state.

Let us start with the conflict that RTE faces within the system. It lies in relations between elementary, secondary and higher education. Discussion of RTE tends to focus on primary and upper-primary education, treating these stages in isolation from other stages of education. This tendency precludes us from noticing the impact that secondary and higher education make on primary education. These higher stages not only influence the share of financial resources available for primary education, but also its curriculum and the pedagogic choices made by teachers. These deeper impacts become accessible for analysis only if we view the system of education in its entirety, focusing on the interaction that occurs between different stages. This interaction is necessarily dominated by higher stages of education which are more directly linked to the economy than the primary stage. On account of this link, the higher stages are seen as being more crucial for national and social development. In this perception, primary education serves mainly as a passage to higher stages. Its own conditions, characteristics and demands tend to be ignored.

India's secondary education is marked by two public examinations. The first one is taken at the end of Class X and the other at the end of Class XII. Both exams are conducted by a 'Board'—a body authorised to certify that a child has passed an exam. The certificate given by this body after the Class X exam also carries the date of birth of the child. The value of a Class X exam, or 'matriculate' exam as it was traditionally called in colonial days, is far greater as a legally recognised certificate of age than as a certifier of academic performance. In this latter role, the Class X Board certificate is mainly a licence to proceed to Classes XI and XII, constituting the 'higher secondary' stage at the end of which comes the second Board exam. A child's performance in this latter exam serves as the basis of entry to an undergraduate college. The main difference between the two exams is that the XII exam is confined to subjects selected by a child whereas the X exam is in all school subjects. This dual-exam system has been known in policy parlance as the 10+2 system, named as such by the Kothari Commission (1964–66). Historically, the Class X exam acted as a filter, serving to stop a vast proportion of children from proceeding either towards college education or a job. This it did by declaring them 'fail'. For a long time, starting with the late nineteenth century, success in the matriculate exam meant eligibility for many different kinds of jobs, including office jobs. By categorising the examinees into 'pass' and 'fail', the matriculation exam result acted as a regulator of upward mobility, both within the system of education and in the job market.

This regulatory function was performed with the help of a marking system that has persisted. The evaluator assigned marks to the answers given by an examinee to the questions given, depending on how 'correct' the answer was. Correctness was judged with reference to an authorised text in most subjects. While this practice was not unique to the Indian subcontinent, the criterion used for determining correctness was peculiar to the colonised societies where the prescribed textbooks for each subject served as the basis for judging the examinee's answer, its correctness and quality. The prescribed textbook served key pedagogic and administrative functions as it controlled the teacher by laying out officially approved knowledge, and controlled the student by indicating how an answer will be judged in a public exam where the identities of the student and the evaluator were treated as confidential, apparently to ensure objectivity or fairness in marking (Kumar 1988; Altbach and Kelly 1988).

The Board exam system has retained these features to the present day. They ensure apparent parity among examinees and thereby equality of opportunity of success among a vast number of children whose economic and social backgrounds are sharply diverse and unequal. The Board exam equalises their chances of success by imposing a strict uniformity on how they can approach the questions set for them and how the evaluator will mark their answers. This exam-centric uniformity is a structural provision in the system of schooling. A major symbolic function served by this uniformity is to signal complete fairness with reference to the hierarchies entrenched in the social structure.

If we look back at the distinctive features of RTE, they all point towards the importance of the teacher's capacity to observe and relate to children individually, recognising individual differences and viewing these differences as a means to build a rich and inclusive pedagogic ethos in the classroom. Section V of RTE covers the staple of a child-centric, experience-oriented teaching strategy. The RTE teacher is someone who knows how to evaluate each child's progress in terms of the child's own growth trajectory, rather than, exclusively, by the old method of comparing each child with others. Moreover, RTE seeks to replace the old once-in-a-year exam system, designed to 'pass' or 'fail', with CCE which allows each child to do things at his or her own pace. There is a fundamental clash between the RTE recipe for cultivating individuality and the secondary level Board exam. The latter imposes uniformity of conditions in order to test each candidate's preparedness for the exam. The source of knowledge used to judge preparedness is the prescribed textbook. RTE's perspective is quite contrary to such a delimitation of knowledge. Not surprisingly, RTE explicitly refers to the National Curriculum Framework (NCF) as the guiding document for academic decisions (NCERT 2005). This document articulates five basic principles on which it is based, the third one being that 'learning must go beyond the textbook'.

This and all other ideas and practices endorsed in the NCF 2005 point towards the same kinds of reforms in curriculum, pedagogy and evaluation that RTE points towards. RTE's enumeration of the characteristics to be found in elementary-classroom teaching and ethos carries a clear rejection of prevailing practices and policies that uphold them. These prevailing practices emphasise uniformity of learning and regimentation of behaviour at the primary level. Uniformity is achieved through textbook-centred teaching, and regimentation through the exam system. Thus, each child is 'prepared' for facing the Board exams from the beginning. Children's individuality is ironed out at the primary stage itself. They progress towards secondary classes mainly by competing with each other. Finally, when the Class X Board exam results are declared, a vast proportion of those who appeared are placed in the 'fail' category, and only the rest are allowed to proceed to the next level, at the end of which they will face another Board exam whose result will decide their chances of going to college and the type of college they will go to if they 'pass'.

The failure rate in the Class X Board exam has been high. In some states, more than fifty per cent of the children appearing in this exam each year 'fail'. As Nawani (2018) shows through her analysis, the rate of failure has been consistently high since colonial times. The 'pass–fail' system has made a significant contribution to the stability that the system has enjoyed over time. Over the recent years, the demand to replace the RTE's provision for CCE with the old 'pass–fail' system of an annual exam, especially at Classes V and VIII levels, has been growing. Those who make this demand, including many state governments, apparently see RTE merely as a law to compel enrolment, not a law that seeks to reform elementary education in order to make the system more equitable. Between RTE's promise of universality and its potential to lay the foundations of greater equality, the former imperative enjoys greater popularity.

Teacher Training and Higher Education

Let us now turn to the relationship between elementary schooling and higher education. This relationship finds expression in teacher training. Preparing teachers through formal training has posed several specific difficulties for India. Let us analyse some of these difficulties with reference to the expectations encoded in RTE. The RTE Act has arrived at a time when India is negotiating the contrary pulls of a welfare-oriented, state-dominated inheritance of economic policy on the one hand, and the pressure to conform to the market-driven model of neo-liberal economics on the other. These contrasting pulls manifested in teacher-training more than a decade before RTE was designed and promulgated. A major change in the teacher-training sector came in the mid-1990s when the National Council for Teacher Education (NCTE) was given the status of a statutory regulatory organisation. Its powers were defined in the NCTE Act passed by the parliament in 1995. These included licensing of institutions giving teacher-training courses, laying down the curriculum and institutional norms, and deciding on the eligibility criteria for recruitment of teachers. This was evidently a huge mandate.

As a commission appointed by the Supreme Court, under the Chairpersonship of the late Chief Justice J. S. Verma, concluded in 2012, NCTE could not fulfil this mandate; instead, it fell victim to commercial interests and functional impediments that led to distortion and large-scale corruption in the training sector (MHRD 2012). Going by the vast amount of documentation this commission produced while presenting its analysis and recommendations for reform, we can say that teacher training represents a highly disturbed area of the system of education in India.

Having failed to overcome older impediments, it has been further injured by new ones arising from the socio-economic landscape. The older impediments included academic poverty of courses and institutions, their aloofness from institutions of higher learning and research, and a sharp division between training for primary and secondary classes. These features had given a highly mechanistic character to teacher training in the colonial period. Post-Independence growth in the sector coincided with the global influence of behaviourism in school pedagogy. The mechanistic disposition of teacher training was encouraged by this influence. Modernisation took the form of self-reassured instrumentalism which found a fertile ground in the textbook-cum-exam culture discussed earlier. By substituting the term 'teacher training' with 'teacher education', NCTE attempted to convey its intention to academise the sector. But new impediments were fast joining the older ones when NCTE started performing its regulatory role with its all-powerful statutory status.

The new problems teacher training faces are mainly three: commercialism or unbridled privatisation, technology-driven neo-behaviourist influence in training institutions as well as in schools, and enfeeblement of higher education affecting the quality of entrants to teacher-training courses. The first of these, namely commercialisation, has proved the hardest to tackle. Starting a private college of teacher training, when compared to engineering or medical college, carries the attraction of high income without much investment. Small- and middle-range entrepreneurs, including politicians, find teacher training a lucrative sector. NCTE's attempt to control the vast number of private institutes by imposing its norms and ensuring compliance by sending inspection teams failed to achieve its purpose and backfired as the Verma Commission noted. Phenomena like 'non-attending' students and underpaid faculty have taken numerous bizarre forms over the years. NCTE has recently doubled the period and quantum of the curriculum of the secondary-level Bachelor of Education (B.Ed.) course. For some of the two thousand private institutes in the B.Ed. business, the new two-year course format initially dampened the demand, but in general the doubling of duration has meant greater income from fee. For the elementary level, there are two main courses, the two-year Diploma in Elementary Education (D.El.Ed.) and the four-year Bachelor Elementary Education (B.El.Ed.)—a less common, innovative programme initiated in the mid-1990s in Delhi University. The latter has not expanded much, mainly because it leads to the same salary and status in the school system as the shorter D.El.Ed. does. The D.El.Ed. has suffered in hundreds of institutions across the country, as has the B.Ed., from practices like proxy infrastructure and non-attending students. The Verma Commission was set up by the Supreme Court in response to a plea against a vast number of bogus D.El.Ed. institutions operating in Maharashtra alone. The Commission examined this allegation, found it to be true, and ordered the closure of the institutions in Maharashtra while presenting its voluminous, futuristic recommendations for the country as a whole. Laudable steps were initiated, but in a few years the regulatory drive through greater surveillance overshadowed the larger, especially academic, reform agenda. The new course structure and guidelines prepared by NCTE have not succeeded in addressing the core problem arising from the uninspiring ethos that Gupta (2018) has described in detail and depth.

Pedagogy Market

A new problem that teacher training faces is the growing influence of neo-behaviourist ideas about learning and their corollaries in teaching. These ideas are shaping the new culture and ethos of both schools and training institutions, pulling them in a direction rather sharply contrary to the one so emphatically and clearly chalked out by RTE. Educational technology has radically grown in terms of what it means and the scope of functions and services it offers to institutions at different levels. What was earlier seen as as equipment to enhance the teacher's capacity for dealing with different kinds of knowledge and activities has burgeoned into a vast repertoire of new meanings of learning and approaches to these new meanings.

This deep change is associated with the arrival of Information and Communication Technology (ICT) and the emergence of what CIO Staff (2003) call the 'new technological environment'. Its impact on education, both as a concept and as an institutionalised system of teaching the young, is difficult to analyse and assess even in countries where the 'pedagogy market' (Kumar 2012) is far more evolved than it is in India at present. What we can notice with certainty is the revivalist influence it has exercised on the behaviourist theories and approaches to learning. Riding the wave of computer-based learning systems, the neo-behaviourist discourse has retrieved the ground it had lost in many countries to the constructivist view of learning and the pedagogical approaches consistent with it. In India, the constructivist view received policy acceptance much later than in other parts of the world. NCF 2005 endorses constructivist learning and explicitly critiques behaviourism and its continuing dominance in Indian classrooms and the examination system. The key difference explained in NCF 2005 is that according to the constructivist view, children form knowledge from their own experience, whereas behaviourism stresses the role played by planned incentives, the setting of common standards or levels and specified routines to negotiate them. Debate on the relative merits of the two perspectives intensified after the promulgation of RTE, which endorses constructivism and NCF 2005, but the ground reality has proved resistant to the constructivist approach.

In teacher training too, the NCTE supported a shift from behaviourist to constructivist pedagogy in a 2009 document called the National Curriculum Framework for Teacher Education (NCFTE).

These indications of consensus notwithstanding, systemic rootedness in behaviourist approaches has proved difficult to nudge. This is quite evident from the ongoing gap between the two powerful institutions that shape educational discourse in India, namely the NCERT and the Central Board of Secondary Education (CBSE). While the former's position became amply clear in NCF 2005, the latter's role of conducting the crucial public exams after Classes X and XII continued to be shaped by the classification of educational objectives presented in Bloom's taxonomy (Bloom 1956). The same can be said about yet another influential body, the Kendriya Vidyalaya Sangathan (KVS), which monitors its over 1000 schools with the nomenclature used in Bloom's taxonomy and the routine classroom tests designed according to this nomenclature. The opposition to RTE-endorsed CCE and the plea for a return to the exam system discussed earlier are also indicative of the continued dominance of the behaviourist perspective.

The 'new technological environment' has further consolidated this dominance. A range of new devices and equipment has been promoted in the growing and diversified network of private schools. The range includes devices such as 'smart' classrooms, computer labs, security and surveillance devices like CCTVs and administrative devices such as fingerprint-based attendance machines. Many private schools now offer a child-tracking facility to parents while their ward is at school. Internet-based learning materials, mobile phones with various networking and recording facilities, and laptops constitute the 'new technological environment'. Though this environment is far more visible in high-end private schools, the state-run schools are also being pushed to create such an environment. State governments in Uttar Pradesh and Rajasthan have distributed free laptops as a symbol of their recognition of talent among the poor.

The understandable gap between the private and government schools on how many technological devices they possess and use is hardly the issue we want to focus on here. This real issue is the nature of the impact of techno-driven changes on learning in elementary, especially primary, schools. NCF 2005 emphasises the importance of hands-on experience for child-centred teaching. The National Focus

Group on Educational Technology, set up under the auspices of NCF 2005, also took a sceptical view of the usefulness of ICT in primary classes (NCERT 2006). The position paper of this group also noted the tendency in the Indian education system to treat technology as a panacea rather than as an aid. This kind of counsel has, however, proved incapable of arousing a debate on ICT in schools. Pressure of the market and state departments themselves have proved much too strong for any debate or policy to emerge. This is, of course, not a uniquely Indian problem. The ICT industry treats educational institutions as a vast captive market. Research on the impact of ICT-rich teaching on children's learning calls for scepticism and caution (OECD 2015), but the power of the 'new technological environment' is far greater than the potential influence of research.

In the context of teacher training too, ICT-based solutions have enjoyed great popularity and favour from policy makers. The pupil-teacher ratio norm laid down in RTE implies a huge backlog of trained teachers. Distance-education courses have been mooted to overcome this gap. The quality of training these courses provide has been questioned within policy-making circles, but the lure of such solutions has proved irresistible. In old-style teacher-training institutions too, expenditure on purchase of ICT equipment has taken precedence over all other expenditure, including expenditure on the hiring of the teaching faculty, libraries and science labs. ICT is seen as an all-purpose remedy for the problems of teacher training. In any case, training for the use of ICT seems more palpable than training for fulfilling the child-centric vision of RTE through reflective teaching, capable of imparting the capacity to inquire to every child.

Relation with Higher Education

Teacher training constitutes an important factor in any educational reform process, but its own health and capacity to contribute to educational reform depends on its relation with higher education. This condition needs to be examined by looking at higher education as the resource from which teachers' claim to eligibility for teaching comes. Teachers of the elementary stage of school education have traditionally comprised two kinds of candidates. Those hired for the primary level are conventionally required to have secondary school qualification, and the ones hired for the upper-primary grades are required to possess a bachelor's degree. Of late, candidates for primary level are also appearing with a bachelor's degree. This is partly a reflection of graduate unemployment, but it is also receiving policy backup, rooted in the view that teachers of primary-level children also need college-level qualifications (NCTE 2010).

Even if a certain proportion of teachers coming into primary-school teaching continues to have pre-degree qualification, the role of higher education in shaping their quality and orientation cannot be denied, because those who taught them at the secondary and higher-secondary levels had to have college or university qualifications. The supply of candidates with college education to training institutions is a major determinant of the contribution that training can make to their subject knowledge acquired at college. Refinement of this knowledge and addition of pedagogic capacities are possible during training if the knowledge of the subject a teacher is going to teach is of a certain acceptable quality. A training institution can hardly start from scratch and impart subject knowledge afresh before introducing trainees to child psychology and other areas of educational theory and pedagogy. This is why the crisis that higher education in India has been going through is of direct relevance to the implementation of RTE. This crisis has been examined and delineated from several perspectives over the years. The crisis has been looked at in terms of financial resources, administrative problems, the question of quality and that of employment of educated youth (Yash Pal 2009). The Verma Commission noted the aloofness of teacher training from higher academic learning and research, treating it as a major reason for its poor quality. It recommended that teacher training for all stages should be considered an area of higher education.

Governance Ethics and the Post-Welfare State

The term 'post-welfare state' refers to the current phase of political economy in India which started in the late 1980s. It is associated with the radical shift of direction in economic policy that took place following a fiscal crisis which the federal government had to address at the end of the 1980s. In popular discourse, the period following this crisis is referred to as the era of economic reforms in the direction of globalisation, liberalisation and privatisation (Corbridge, Harriss and Jeffrey 2013; Kurien 1994). Liberalisation included opening the Indian economy to foreign capital and the broadening of opportunities for private business in traditionally state-controlled sectors, such as education, including higher as well as school education and health. According to many observers, these economic trends altered India's general political ethos, narrowing the space available for liberal-minded discourses and dialogue in different spheres, including the economy itself. The post-Independence consensus on welfarism eroded even as private finance intensified its hold on two key welfare sectors—education and health. The discourse of 'governance' gained popularity, confining the state's role to regulation or overseeing. Its gradual withdrawal from direct involvement in education in order to enable private capital to have greater room was celebrated as a sign of evolution, supposedly marking the end of bureaucratic control and political interference.

The earliest signs of this general transition became visible in the difference between the 1986 National Policy on Education (NPE) and the Programme of Action (PoA) released in 1992. This was the period when the discourse of economic reforms favouring private capital, both domestic and foreign, acquired a palpable shape. The PoA attempted to adjust the NPE to the new economic scenario that had emerged rather dramatically in 1991, following the acceptance of the 'structural adjustment programme' by the new central government. India's 'adjustment' to the regimen of global corporate capital and international donor institutions marked a significant change in the self-identity of the state and its role. The term 'post-welfare state' is meant to connote this change. It is preferable to the more widely used term, that is, the 'neo-liberal state', because the latter demands considerable familiarity with the history of liberalism and its various discourses. Also, 'neo-liberalism' is now commonly used to point towards a global reality, hence it strengthens the assumed lack of any significant distinctions or specificities among different nations. In the context of India's state, which was formed under colonial rule, the current phase of economic growth is characterised by the transfer of several functions and responsibilities to managerial experts representing corporate capital. The transfer of the state's educational responsibilities is occurring in the name of efficiency. Private profit is not involved in every case of institutional or functional transfer as a considerable amount of philanthropic capital is being garnered for investment in education. Political correctness helps philanthropy to be assigned educational responsibilities of various kinds without the risk of democratic murmur; yet, the transfer involves a shift of these responsibilities from democratic to managerial space. This kind of shift is best expressed by the term 'post-welfare state', which sheds its own welfare role in an ethos that permits political consensus to emerge on a change in the basic functions of the state.

One might ask whether the Indian state, originally formed under colonial rule, was a truly welfare state at any point. Such a question can best be answered by referring to the Constitution which conveys an aspiration to create a welfare society and state in India. Such an aspiration is articulated through a transformative vision and values including social justice and equality of rights. We can notice a welfarist inclination in the policies followed in education during the initial decades following Independence, even though these policies were not backed by adequate financial provisions. The last expression of such an inclination can be seen in the 1986 policy on education. As explained below, it was soon going to be reviewed and recast in a different mode, adjusting to the emerging demands of entrepreneurial forces that saw in education a vast area of profit-making opportunities and sale of commodities. An external, global ethos in favour of such a shift already existed by then as scholars such as Tomlinson (2001) and Slaughter and Leslie (1991) have demonstrated.

After RTE was passed by the parliament, as a federal law, it was assumed that the central government will carry a major part of the financial demand RTE's implementation will put on the states.

Initially, this process was seen as a natural progression from the SSA, a national flagship programme led by federal and federally mediated international funds. However, after the tapering off of SSA funds in 2013, the central government chose to view RTE's implementation as a responsibility of the states. In many states, this responsibility is being outsourced to corporate capital and non-government organisations (Nambissan and Ball 2010). For corporate money, the use of technology for distance-training programmes has proved an attractive option. It involves massive supplies of equipment. Schools represent a mega-space for business, not merely in pedagogic equipment and material, but also in surveillance technology like CCTVs. Public–private partnership policy has played a key role in inaugurating the incorporation of state-run schools into a vast market of goods and services. This process has enabled a corporate-managerial culture to govern school administration and classroom transactions. 'Outcome'-oriented teaching is a pivotal aspect of this new policy ethos. It demands teachers confine their role to implementing a pre-scripted curriculum which is tied to regular testing. Their training for an outcome-focused pedagogy helps them to view learning mainly in terms of preparation for tests. Terms like 'efficiency' and 'accountability' provide the justification for this regimen of test-oriented teaching. It enables teachers to ignore the humanistic assumptions and agenda of RTE and the concept of quality associated with these goals. If the RTE Act is amended to facilitate the return of annual exams, it will further encourage the reversal of RTE's reform agenda.

The focus of that agenda was to create room for the child's agency and enhance teachers' capacity to recognise that agency. In a highly stratified and patriarchal society like ours, recognition of the child's agency implies overcoming one's own assumptions and biases about caste, gender, class and religion. This is a tall order for the teacher. In India's case, RTE's agenda to make elementary education child-centric means a radical shift in acceptance of children as a social category (Kumar 2016). Teachers' acceptance of such a category and its inclusive span depends on how well teachers are prepared through their own education and training to view their role in society and how clear they are about the meaning of learning as experience. RTE calls for teachers who do not use fear of failure or corporal punishment to motivate children. RTE will make an impact on social inequality if teachers are clear about their professional responsibility to create an ethos in which children experience dignity and autonomy. For a Dalit child or a girl, equality is a function of the everyday experience of learning in an ethos of dignity and comfort. Test scores do not ensure a sense of equality, nor does outcome-centric teaching mean efficiency for a social goal like equality. This is why the current emphasis on tangible outcomes and accountability is misplaced and hollow. It can at best promote universal attendance, not an experience of learning that enables children to absorb dignity as an essential ingredient of equality. A narrow interpretation of RTE is also promoted, perhaps inadvertently, by those lobbying for specific causes. They focus on implementation of RTE in a purely administrative sense even if that means overlooking, even reversing, the space RTE creates for dignity of the child and the teacher of young children. At times, such a demand translates into encouraging the state's abdication of its responsibility towards elementary education and handing it over to non-government organisations, including those representing corporate interests. This is indeed a highly confusing ethos for a complex law such as RTE to move towards becoming a social reality. The least one can say is that the ethos is no less confusing now than it was before RTE was drafted and passed by parliament. RTE signifies one among the many paradoxical attainments of Indian democracy in its struggle to engage with deep social divisions and the state's colonial heritage of reluctant acceptance of its social duties.

References

Altbach, Philip. G, and Gail Paradise Kelly. 1988. *Textbooks in the Third World: Policy, Content and Context*. Garland Reference Library of Social Science. London: Routledge.

Bloom, Benjamin S. 1956. *Taxonomy of Educational Objectives, Vol. 1.* New York: David McKay.

CIO Staff. 2003. 'David Elkind: Technology's Impact on Child Growth and Development.' *CIO.com*. Accessed 15 January 2020. https://www.cio.com/article/2441936/david-elkind--technology-s-impact-on-child-growth-and-development.html.

Corbridge, Stuart, John Harriss, and Craig Jeffrey. 2013. *Understanding India: Politics, Economy and Society*. Cambridge: Polity Press.

Gupta, Latika. 2018. 'The Discourse of Teacher Education in India.' In *Routledge Handbook of Education in India*, edited by Krishna Kumar, 179–88. London: Routledge.

Kobayashi, Tetsuya. 1976. *Society, Schools, and Progress in Japan*. New York: Pergamon Press.

Kumar, Krishna. 1988. 'Origins of India's Textbook Culture.' *Comparative Education Review* 32(4): 452–64.

Kumar, Krishna. 2012. 'CBSE-Pearson Tie-up: Pedagogy Market.' *Economic and Political Weekly* 47: 47–48.

Kumar, Krishna. 2016. 'Studying Childhood in India'. *Economic and Political Weekly* (51: 23) https://www.epw.in/journal/2016/23/commentary/studying-childhood-india.html.

Kurien, C. T. 1994. *Global Capitalism and the Indian Economy*. New Delhi: Orient Longman.

Lawson, John, and Harold Silver. 1973. *A Social History of Education in England*. London: Methuen.

Mehendale, Archana. 2018. 'Compulsion to Educate.' In *Routledge Handbook of Education in India*, edited by Krishna Kumar, 13–25. London: Routledge.

MHRD (Ministry of Human Resource Development). 2012. *Justice Verma Commission on Teacher Education*. New Delhi: MHRD.

Moore, Barrington Jr. 1968. *Social Origins of Democracy and Dictatorship*. Boston: Beacon Press.

Naik, J. P. 1975. *Elementary Education in India: A Promise to Keep*. New Delhi: Allied.

Nambissan, Geetha B. 2009. *Exclusion and Discrimination in Schools*. New Delhi: Institute of Dalit Studies and UNICEF.

Nambissan, Geetha B., and Stephen J. Ball. 2010. 'Advocacy Networks, Choice and Private Schooling of the Poor in India.' *Global Networks* 10(3): 324–43. doi:10.1111/j.1471-0374.2010.00291.x.

Nawani, Disha. 2018. 'Examination for Elimination.' In *Routledge Handbook of Education in India*, edited by Krishna Kumar, 64–78. London: Routledge.

NCERT. 2005. *National Curriculum Framework*. New Delhi: NCERT.

NCERT. 2006. *National Focus Group Position Paper on Educational Technology*. New Delhi: NCERT.

NCTE. 2010. *National Curriculum Framework for Teacher Education*. New Delhi: NCTE.

OECD. 2015. *Students, Computers and Learning*. Paris: OECD.

Slaughter, Sheila, and Larry L. Leslie. 1997. *Academic Capitalism*. Baltimore: Johns Hopkins University Press.

Tomlinson, Sally. 2001. *Education and the Post-Welfare Society*. Buckingham: Open University Press.

Touraine, Alain. 1998. 'Social Transformations of the Twentieth Century.' *International Social Science Journal*, 443–57.

Weiner, Myron. 1991. *The Child and the State in India*. Delhi: Oxford.

Yash Pal Committee Report. 2009. 'Renovation and Rejuvenation of Higher Education.' MHRD.

7

Education and Poverty

This is an adapted version of a lecture delivered in 2013 at the National Institute of Open Schooling (NIOS) to mark its silver jubilee.

In a society where poverty is far more common than prosperity, one would expect the implications of poverty for education to be widely recognised. What we find, instead, is that poverty is seldom mentioned directly in policy documents on education. Policy makers feel more comfortable using euphemisms like 'economically weaker sections', the 'marginalised' or the 'deprived' to refer to the poor. No wonder the impact of poverty on children's life at school and learning is understood rather vaguely. This is true of educational planners, school administrators as well as teachers. Problems faced by children of the poor are discussed as 'their' problems, not as institutional or national problems. Quite often, these problems are cited as individual issues. In this way, they get minimised, both in scale and gravity.

The reason why poverty must be treated as a factor of education arises from a basic incompatibility between the two. Education necessarily demands long-term horizons. Poverty, on the contrary, compels people to remain embedded in immediate or short-term concerns. India has now recognised eight years of compulsory education as a fundamental right of every child. The parliament has passed a law to enforce this right. However, endemic poverty and social inequality are posing tough constraints in making this law a reality. Moreover, elementary education by itself means little; it can only serve as a beginning for further education over many years. The intellectual and economic value of education depends on the length of time for which participation in the life of an institution has been sustained, and also on how substantial this participation is. The informal economy on which the overwhelming majority of the poor survive forces them to live from day to day. They want to—but usually fail to—plan for the distant future in which their progeny might reap the fruits of education. The children belonging to poor families find it difficult to cope with the regularity that schools demand. This is because hunger, illness and insecurity interrupt their life at home all the time. Their parents have to use most of their energies in order to deal with everyday emergencies.

Life under poverty is unpredictable and prone to sudden losses and traumas. For the poor, there is no such thing as normalcy. Anything can happen anytime, and all they can do is to cope as they suffer. In big cities, municipal authorities can suddenly clear a street of food vendors or bulldoze an unauthorised colony where the poor live. The next morning, when a child fails to be at school or looks subdued, teachers show little curiosity to find out what might have happened to the child's father or mother the previous afternoon or how the family spent the night. Rural life has similar uncertainties. Flood waters can drown hundreds of houses; yet a school located in a flood-affected village is supposed to function and cover the prescribed syllabus in stipulated time, like any other school. Construction of dams or factories can mean the forced displacement of whole villages. What will happen to children is the least important concern for those in charge of such operations. I once met children in Manibeli, a village that now lies at the bottom of the Sardar Sarovar Dam in Gujarat. These children had gone through the trauma of seeing their school vanish under water. At the new school where they had been accommodated, no one was interested in understanding the trauma they had suffered.

These are examples of dramatic changes that poverty can bring in the lives of children. But the routine effects of poverty are no less significant. Let us take the example of the corrosive impact of poverty on children's health and mental capacities. Frequent illness, especially on account of stomach-related problems, is common among children who live in conditions characterised by poor sanitation. Studies have shown how filthy surroundings, in which faecal material mixes with water and food, weaken the capacity to absorb nutrition. Limited resources to eat well and regularly result in a daily cycle of anxiety and low energy which translates into poor attention to the teacher's expectations. There cannot be better evidence of the relationship between hunger and education than the success of the mid-day meals programme. The fact that this minimalist scheme has actually improved enrolment and retention proves how major a role hunger and malnourishment play in pushing children to drop out of school. Certain state governments have administered a dose of deworming medicine, recognising the prevalence of parasites and the impact of this condition on children's nutritional status, energy and attention. However, a one-time treatment of such persistent medical conditions can hardly make a long-term difference. In addition to stomach ailments caused by unclean water, urban poverty now faces the common spectre of air pollution. Its impact on children's lungs and the effects of low oxygen in the air on their intellectual growth have barely received recognition.

Let us now turn to the better understood economic issues. Poverty usually leads to children's involvement in household work and outside activities that might augment the family's income. Children engage in these activities on top of their school work. The burden of responsibilities at home or outside directly influences children's participation in school life and their capacity to fulfil the teacher's expectations. Teachers of private schools where twenty-five per cent of the seats are now being given to the 'economically weaker sections' (EWS) category seldom know with clarity what life at home means for children in this category. From looking after younger siblings to sweeping the floor and cooking, an EWS girl often shares all major domestic tasks her mother is supposed to accomplish on a daily basis. Whether children work at home or outside, their effort to juggle work-related responsibilities with classroom routines makes their life at school porous and thin. Absence from school or inability to focus has a direct impact on performance. Once a child starts to lag behind others, he or she becomes an object of stereotyping by classmates and teachers. A vicious cycle sets in. Common stereotypes about the poor get invoked in the teacher's mind and the child's behaviour resonates and reinforces these stereotypes. Some of these stereotypes are rooted in caste-related beliefs or in religion. Of course, no principal or teacher would ever acknowledge being guided by these stereotypes. Caste, religion, habitation and poverty make a complex social compound that teachers are not trained to recognise or analyse. Gender adds yet another dimension of complexity to this compound. Indian teachers, in any case, work under trying and burdensome conditions that leave little scope for reflection on individual children.

All over the world, scholars have pointed out that education alone cannot address poverty. However, it holds an important place among the numerous strategies that a welfare state can adopt to loosen the grip that chronic poverty has on its victims. A recent British study led by Anand Mani[1] shows how poverty saps its victims of energy. They often fail to keep up with the effort required to avail themselves of the state's benefits. The daily struggles and anxieties of life reinforce the cycle of ill health and missed appointments. In India, the state's efforts are quite often symbolic. A good example of this is the distribution of iron tablets or syrup to overcome chronic malnutrition among adolescent girls. Had the famous mid-day meal been aimed at middle-class children, it would have been priced more realistically. Greater flexibility to cope with price rise would have been permitted. Schemes for the poor are themselves so emaciated and stiff that they cannot be expected to make a significant difference in the lives of their beneficiaries. Even when efficiently run, such schemes provide just a thin cushion for children of the poor to cope with their harsh daily lives.

Another common weakness one can notice in strategies to combat poverty is that they are not sufficiently contextualised or flexible. Rigidity and uniformity are believed to be necessary to avoid corruption and misuse. Even a distinction as broad as 'rural' and 'urban' is overlooked when plans to address the educational problems of poor children are designed. Whether a school has drowned in a dam or been blasted by insurgents or demolished because it was collapsing anyhow, the officials in charge make no distinction or find ways to compensate for the loss of classes. Nowadays, children studying in government schools are deemed to be poor and, therefore, unimportant. I remember visiting a village in Haryana where the children told me that their best teacher had been transferred two months ahead of the annual examination. All over the country, government school children cope with the absence of their teachers during elections. No private school shares this peculiar burden of democracy. It is the children studying in government schools who subsidise the cost involved in the smooth conduct of elections while their parents enthusiastically cast their vote, hoping that it will lead to improvement in their lives.

Although education alone cannot alleviate the effects of poverty, teachers can make a significant difference in the educational experience of poor children. This can happen only if the training of teachers equips them with the awareness of what poverty means. Our training programmes are so wordy, wasteful and devoid of academic depth, they are in no position to make an effort to engage with specific problems like poverty. Furthermore, a widespread belief in the ideology of social Darwinism prevents both teachers and their trainers from realising that children of the poor are like any other group of children, with individual differences of interest and motivation. According to this ideology, survival is proof of being the fittest, hence only the exceptional child from a poor family is endowed by nature to succeed. Training courses don't engage with such attitudes and beliefs. The Right to Education Act has forced private schools to accept a certain degree of social mixing. However, teachers who work in mixed classrooms don't expect all children to succeed in their own different ways. They focus on the few who look exceptional; the rest are believed to lack any potential. It is hardly surprising that the system of education makes so little impact on the majority of children from poorer backgrounds.

NOTE

1. The study is discussed in the 2013 article 'Poverty Saps Mental Capacity to Deal with Complex Tasks, Say Scientists', written by Alok Jha and published by *The Guardian*.

8

The Death of a Small Boy

A version of this article appeared in The Hindu *on 18 December 2012.*

Picture a small boy facing two adult men. They are furious over something they suspect he has done, so they start hitting him. They feel they have the authority to do so because they are teachers. The boy is absolutely helpless. It hardly matters whether he is upper caste or Dalit or tribal. It is his isolation that matters in this moment of his helplessness. In this moment, he stands beyond the reach of all the institutional mechanisms set up to protect him from the violent fate that awaits him. Neither the UN Convention on the Rights of the Child (UNCRC) nor the National Commission for Protection of Child Rights (NCPCR) can rescue him. In any case, the state cannot be of much help, for it is the state under whose authority and supervision the two adults beating him mercilessly have been selected and appointed to serve as teachers. It hardly matters whether they are serving in a government or a private school, for both kinds of schools draw the legitimacy of their access to the child's mind and body from the powers entrusted to the state.

In this instance, the two adults kept thrashing the boy till he collapsed. His parents took him to a hospital in a neighbouring city. The doctors found that his backbone had been smashed. The treatment they suggested was too expensive, so the parents took the boy to a hospital in another city. There, the boy was declared dead. From the report that has appeared in the press, it seems the teachers got angry when the boy informed them that the 'school bucket' had broken, and they suspected he had broken it. This incident occurred in a government school in Betul, Madhya Pradesh. One of the teachers has been arrested, and perhaps the other one will also be taken into police custody soon. The case against them will undoubtedly proceed. Perhaps the NCPCR will back it after its own enquiry. Due procedures will be followed, and the law, as they say, will take its own course. While the case starts its journey along that familiar course, we can ask at least one fresh question, though it is not immediately evident how exactly it should be formulated.

Teachers' Crime?

As a crime, corporal punishment at school offers little scope for any doubt about the culprit. The newly granted Right to Education (RTE) seeks to ban corporal punishment, meaning thereby that a teacher cannot use it as a means of disciplining a child. In a case where corporal punishment has led to injury or death, the teacher's culpability is self-evident. All that a legal enquiry needs to establish is that the punishment was actually given, and that it is this punishment that has led to serious injury or death. In the classroom, the teacher alone has authoritative access to the child's body, and this access derives from the teacher being in charge of the child's mind. As an adult, the teacher gets this physical access on account of the role in which he or she is placed. Let us ask therefore: 'Who places the teacher in this role?' Such a question will allow us to go deeper in our investigation of those culpable for the crime suffered by the child.

The last two decades have witnessed a dramatic change in the public profile and status of primary-school teachers. While the RTE has improved children's status and the government's image, the person responsible for the child's wellbeing and development at school remains a poor, lowly civil servant. In the specific case of Madhya Pradesh, the economic and social statuses of teachers have undergone major changes as a result of prolonged administrative manoeuvres. It has little to do with shifts in political power and ideology. A series of so-called policy reforms initiated during the Congress regime (1993–2003) have been sustained by the BJP which rules the state at present. The history of change in teachers' lives is intertwined with the larger policy and programme scenario at the national level. During the 1990s, the government chose to restructure the system of education by allowing local groups to start primary schools and by delegating the task of recruiting teachers to the village panchayat. Cadre management policies were changed to accommodate different types of contractual, 'para' appointments. The state decided to treat its existing pool of teachers as a 'dying cadre', implying that no new appointments would be made at the older scales. New teachers were given nominal training and a pittance in the name of emoluments. As the demand for regularising these contractual appointees acquired political profitability, new pay scales were created that were radically lower than the older ones. While other north Indian states acknowledged that there were problems with para-teachers, Madhya Pradesh instead recognised them as full-fledged 'teachers'. Initially, Madhya Pradesh was alone in this remarkable feat of governance; of late Bihar has emulated it by replacing existing teachers as they retire with this new, low-paid breed.

Kaun Banega Teacher?

This brief introduction to a complex history should suffice to indicate that, over the last two decades, a primary school teacher's job has lost what little covetability it had acquired since Independence. It is no more an attractive career for someone who has modest financial ambition and the urge to work with children, together with the aptitude to do so. The selection procedure does not involve the search for necessary attributes and talent, as it is based entirely on credentials which indicate precious little about the person and his or her capacities. Training courses that make a person eligible for recruitment have scant academic or practical worth in terms of the experience they provide. A vast majority of institutions licensed to offer this training are bogus. A commission chaired by Justice J. S. Verma, which was appointed by the Supreme Court, found that only forty-four out of the three hundred institutions in Maharashtra providing a Diploma in Education were qualified to run the course. Such instances can be found in other states as well. The minimum qualification to enter this two-year diploma course for primary-level teaching is Class XII. Apparently, no emotional or intellectual maturity is demanded of the person who will look after and teach six- to eleven-year-olds. In the name of training, young people are required to go through pathetic institutional rituals, in many cases by means of correspondence or distance teaching. Among the courses available for elementary school teacher training, there is just one exception that offers depth of academic and practical experience. This is the four-year Bachelor of Elementary Education (B.El.Ed.) course offered in eight colleges of Delhi University. This remarkable programme deserves expansion and replication, but instead, Delhi University is reportedly planning to start a two-year diploma kind of course to produce primary-school teachers. I wish the university had noticed that such a short duration is just not sufficient to enable trainees to link theory with practise, let alone question their own beliefs and values.

Let us now return to the Betul story. When the legal machinery receives all the evidence it needs to decide culpability in the case of the boy who has died, can we hope that the state's responsibility will also be examined? His teachers who brutally hit him had access to his body *because* they were recruited to serve as teachers. The court must ask on what grounds did the state satisfy itself that such persons could look after the welfare and rights of a small boy. The court must also ask what kind of professional training they were given to perform their role as teachers. Their criminal failure to serve as teachers deserves an explanation. A major part of that explanation lies in the casual approach that the state—as the custodian of children and the nation's human resource—has adopted towards the job of teaching the young. This approach is incompatible with the lofty ideals of the RTE and the Constitution.

9

Leela Dube's Poser

A version of this article appeared in The Hindu *on 30 June 2012 under the title 'A Messy Corner of India's Modernity'.*

A school principal in Melur in the Madurai district of Tamil Nadu is reported to have denied admission to two girls whose parents had married them off after they completed Class X. Prima facie, it seems the principal is wrongly applying her authority. Also, in the broader social context, it seems strange and unacceptable that the benefits of education should be denied to a girl just because she is now a married woman. There are other ways to look at this story. When I read it, I wished Leela Dube, who died last month, were alive and I could phone her to find out what she thought about it. Her view of such matters derived its perspective from a deeper commitment—to social reality, rather than to activism or political correctness. Before I speculate on how she might have responded to the Melur principal's decision, let me recall my pedagogic experience with one of her writings.

Gender is now a common topic in courses on education and teaching. Everyone knows that discrimination on the basis of gender is a major problem in schools. Equally clearly, everyone has figured out how to talk about this problem. Political correctness on this topic has seeped in, all the way to the district- and block-level institutions of teacher training. Resource persons are now readily available in all parts of the country who can wax eloquent about gender parity and how it can be sustained in the classroom. Officers at all levels have equipped themselves with PowerPoint presentations that show how fast the gender gap is shrinking in enrolment, retention and outcomes. The same ease and excitement pervade the media when the Central Board of Secondary Education (CBSE) and other boards declare their Class X and XII results. 'Girls outshine boys' says the banner headline year after year. An ethos pointing to a nice social revolution envelops us. In a happy environment of this kind, how do you ask students to notice the social world stretched right across their daily vision but tightly wrapped up under the pleasant discourse of change shared by the state and the social activist? Faced with this problem, I ask my students to read Leela Dube's paper tersely titled 'On the Construction of Gender: Socialisation of Hindu Girls in Patrilineal India'. Once they read it, they stop being glib, which is no small matter in this age of readiness to recommend.

In this paper, first published in 1988, Leela Dube portrays the cultural imprinting that turns girls into socially acceptable women. The portrait is laboriously drawn, with data and insights acquired from diverse sources and regions. The style is marked by a concern for accuracy and detail, and nowhere is the reader treated as either a concerned citizen or a social reformer. Throughout its forty pages, Leela Dube sticks to her role as a scholar whose primary job is to examine human behaviour and the institutions that shape it. In this case, the institutions are family and kinship. Their joint venture ensures that a little girl starts to learn, from infancy onwards, that it is her destiny to leave her natal home for an uncertain future in a family to which she will belong after marriage. This destiny is cast in the rock of cultural practices, ranging from religious rituals to the everyday language of lullabies, songs, idioms and metaphors. For the single-minded pursuit of matrimony, the girl's appearance, body movements, habits and dispositions are to be honed into the approved model of beauty, self-restraint and self-abnegation. Space and time are supposed to shrink into increasingly narrow corridors of activity, and the natural desire for freedom a girl might have felt as a baby must be dissolved into a regime of responsibility and self-denial.

The essay leaves you wondering whether girls have a childhood at all, or whether they move straight from infancy into adulthood. Secondly, it sets up an explicit conflict between the aims of girls' socialisation at home and their education at school. Tradition and customs require girls to learn during childhood that they must submit to male authority in all aspects of their life. The core of this learning lies in giving up any claim to intellectual autonomy and individual uniqueness. With the full force that religious and caste beliefs—and their representations in mythology—might be expected to carry for the young mind, girls are made to internalise the all-encompassing social value of their bodies for reproduction. Restrictions on physical movement and posture, and on the use of time and space, begin much before puberty, but after menarche these restrictions acquire comprehensive rigour. If we add to them the chronic anxiety about the inescapability of leaving one's parents' home, we can somewhat appreciate how incompatible the norms of girlhood in India are with the basic principles of education. These principles revolve around the child's agency and freedom. Progressive pedagogy is supposed to enhance the child's confidence and courage to develop her identity as an individual. Both in terms of its emotional content and the reasoning on which it is based, the agenda of cultural imprinting of girls' minds contradicts the objectives of child-centred education.

Leela Dube does not hesitate to articulate this conflict: 'Can we really think of reforming the education system to bring about a more "enlightened" relationship between the sexes as long as the larger structures which provide the context for the education system continue to reproduce gender-based relationships of domination and subordination?' Let us attempt to use this perspective to make sense of the news from the government school at Melur. Both girls who are being denied admission to Class XI have studied at this school till Class X. The school and its principal were apparently not taken into account by the parents who arranged their marriage, nor by the larger community which participated in the ceremony. In matters of this kind, we tend to ignore how peripheral the school is to society. It is a place where people send their children to enable them to seek certified qualifications. The school neither forms a point of reference for making decisions, nor does it carry a curriculum relevant to everyday living. Its principal and teachers are perceived as petty functionaries of the government.

In her denial of admission to the two girls who have now become married women, the principal is conveying her inconsequential anger. If we blame her for misusing her authority and compel her to admit these girls—as the Tamil Nadu government will surely do quite soon—we miss the opportunity to listen to a voice we have institutionally muzzled. This is the voice of teachers who are supposed to carry on their lean shoulders the full burden of the rhetoric of national development and social transformation. The enormity of challenges teachers face in their daily professional routine is trivialised by us when we expect them to act like pedagogues and social reformers rolled into one. This latter role constitutes a grand illusion as they can expect to receive no cooperation from the larger society when they try to go against established norms. Curricular policies reduce their intellectual struggle to a ritual, to be observed for the sake of examination success and certification. Indeed, their training as teachers lacks professional rigour and length precisely because both state and society treat them—whatever the rhetoric may be—as minor cogs in the system's wheel. The Melur principal has made the mistake of conveying this a bit too explicitly. She is right in indicating that she is not equipped to run a school for married women. If the government is concerned about the education of child brides, it should develop a curriculum for them and start institutions where it can be taught.

True, such a step will form an oxymoron. The state cannot acknowledge a child bride as an adult citizen with constitutionally endowed rights. She is an ambiguous entity, a progeny of the contradiction between state and society. She inhabits a messy, forgotten corner of India's modernity. We tend to look at her, when we must, with emotion and studied surprise. What distinguished Leela Dube as a social scientist is that she had the courage to stare unemotionally at such dimly lit corners of Indian modernity. About child labour too, she wrote in a similar vein, arguing that it is embedded in the deeper structures of society, not all of which have a purely economic character. When we ignore these structures and act like impatient activists, we inadvertently place ourselves at the disposal of strategists whose interests are narrow and short-term.

As a major scholar of our times, Leela Dube teaches us how to register the present moment in the long story of women's subordination.

On both these matters, Leela Dube's doubts about quick-fix solutions have proved valid. Child marriage continues to be perceived, in certain sections of society, as a way to slow down crimes against women. On child labour, recent changes in legal policy indicate a compromise.

10

Education and Caste

A version of this article appeared in The Indian Express *on 7 July 2018 under the title 'The Curriculum Taboo'.*

A news report from Maharashtra reminds us of why we must keep on engaging with older issues and debates. Even as brave new India forges ahead with smartphones, smart boards and smart cities, caste remains a major force shaping social relations and politics. Three adolescent Dalit boys were brutally assaulted and paraded naked after they were caught swimming in a well forbidden for use by Dalits. The assault was recorded on video. Perpetrators of violence against members of oppressed groups document their acts themselves, apparently to establish their brazenness. Perhaps they also intend to warn others against transgressing traditionally maintained boundaries of upper-caste authority. They don't believe that history has moved on, towards new social norms. There is something in the current political ethos that persuades them to hope for a return to old times.

The episode reminds me of the role that wells used to play in India's social life before the advent of piped water. Wells were often demarcated as caste territories. To have a well of your own, in your courtyard, was a symbol of status. There were public wells too, commemorating the liberal vision of an enlightened authority figure. Several short stories by Premchand portray life around a well and the conflict that wells often witnessed. One poignant example is the story '*Thakur ka kuan*' ('The Thakur's Well'), probably written in the early 1930s. The plot is brief and the end bleak, although violent horror is avoided. An untouchable labourer's wife attempts to fetch water from a Thakur's well. It is dark, and her husband is very ill and thirsty. The well accessible to the untouchables smells rotten because an animal has fallen into it. The labourer's wife knows the terrible risk she is taking, but she goes ahead. Just when she is close to success, she is spotted and runs for her life. When she reaches home, she finds her ill husband drinking the foul water.

Many today would like to believe that the portrait of India this story offers is now obsolete. The Maharashtra incident proves that this is not entirely so. We can debate the exact nature of its relevance, but we can't doubt it. As Premchand's story figures in school and college textbooks in many parts of India, you can hear audio and video lessons on it on the internet. In most of these lessons, students are told to appreciate Premchand's masterly treatment of old social problems like untouchability and superstition. Understanding and appreciation of his craft of fiction is important for getting good marks. The audio teacher insists that social problems like caste discrimination are a thing of the past. If they sometimes manifest today, it is only in remote villages. As expected, the lesson has a moral agenda—to establish that education is fighting against such inhuman practices.

Apart from including such literature in textbooks, education in most states does precious little to deal with caste issues in any depth or detail. Indeed, caste remains a curricular taboo—it is not supposed to be discussed directly. Nor is it acknowledged as a major social institution, shaping relationships as important as marriage. It's not just schools and colleges which avoid engaging with it, but teacher-training institutions too. All that is discussed is the reservation policy and its constitutional aim. The hope that caste prejudices will gradually diminish, if not vanish, is based on general faith in education, rather than on any insight into how education works or how its agency can be deployed on a subject like caste.

If we try to answer two questions on this subject, we might achieve some clarity. The first question is: 'Has education helped to speed up economic and social mobility among the lower-placed castes?' The second question is: 'Has education helped to reduce caste-based prejudice?' The answer to the first question is, 'Yes.' For the second question, one can at best say, 'Maybe, but not much.' Proof of this second answer can be found in many university campuses.

From friendships to politics, the influence of caste can be observed everywhere. Many young people feel undisturbed by it. The rhetoric of being fair, open and unprejudiced is well-established in colleges, but no real learning about caste-based practices and prejudices takes place. The belief persists that including the caste system in the curriculum will only reinforce it. Many schools and colleges are established by caste associations, and they too prefer to let the magic of caste remain subtle, influencing the young mind quietly. The same applies to teacher-training institutes. You cannot persuade people to take the time to read a book as slim as *Indian Society* (National Book Trust), written by the late S. C. Dube to promote informed dialogue about the caste system. Wild ideas and stereotypes nicely co-exist and flourish with revivalist politics which forbid any reference to caste on the grounds that it will spoil the country's image.

Ambedkar was right in seeing caste as a barrier to India's intellectual growth, in addition to being the lever of oppression. His teacher at Columbia, the educational philosopher John Dewey, had given communication a central place in his model of democracy. Ambedkar used the metaphor of social endosmosis to explain how the caste system prevents the flow of ideas and knowledge. Endosmosis ensures the passage of fluid through a membrane to an adjoining cell. The caste system, Ambedkar felt, deprives India of this basic means of social health. Like Dewey, Ambedkar had faith in the power of education to nourish democracy. Our system of education continues to be too weak to promote any kind of endosmosis, even across disciplines, let alone social groups. Someone studying science, engineering or management may never be intellectually challenged for holding casteist views. In routine life, such views reassure colleagues that you are normal. If you are part of the urban middle class, you learn to perceive caste as something remote, even as it permeates your everyday world and gives you an identity.

11

Peasants as Citizens

A version of this article appeared in The Hindu *on 3 July 2017 under the title 'Written-off in the Hinterland'.*

Rural Mandsaur, where five persons were killed during a demonstration, is a prosperous region of western Madhya Pradesh. More than a decade ago, I had the opportunity of spending two days with children of a private residential school in Mandsaur. At the time, it was the only English-medium residential school in the area. Its vast and opulent campus in the middle of sprawling green fields was a great anomaly. The school had little to do with its milieu. It represented the dream of a philanthropist to export the best human talent of his region to the global market. This dream resonated national policy trends which, since the mid-1980s, had chosen to view education mainly as human resource development. The idea that education can serve a village in ways that allow it to retain its best boys and girls had been discarded long ago. If you carried in your mind any residue of Gandhi's ideas about village education, you would see the residential academy in rural Mandsaur as an incongruity. Here was an institution set up to give its metropolitan counterparts stiff competition on global playgrounds. The school had invested heavily in computers. Its strategy to serve rural children was neither purely commercial nor patronising. It was a professional bid to give rural youth an opportunity to aspire to legitimate heights. Some of them belonged to well-off farming families who could afford to send them to study in a residential school. But there were quite a few whose parents had small landholdings or minor jobs. For them, the school meant a potential break from the likelihood of a life dependent on shrinking income from agriculture and labour.

The impact of education on rural life has remained consistent since colonial days. When a village boy did well at school, he was expected to shift to a nearby town. That is where he could expect his talent to be recognised. Gradually, villages became the supplier of talent to the towns and cities. Only those who were dependent on land stayed back. With the passage of time, land was subdivided into smaller pieces, making agriculture unattractive. In recent times, investments have made land more productive, but real income has declined. Work opportunities in villages in non-agricultural pursuits remained scarce, and in the recent past, job growth has come to a standstill. The phenomenon of 'waiting' to find work, described by Craig Jeffrey (in *Indian Village: A Conceptual History*) in the context of Uttarakhand and western Uttar Pradesh, is valid elsewhere too. One part of this phenomenon is the struggle to sustain one's aspirations and the other part is living with frustration.

It is quite common these days among parents in all districts of Madhya Pradesh to send their sons and daughters to towns like Bhopal and Indore for coaching. As a broad-spectrum industry, coaching now represents an acceptable way of spending much of your youth. It fills time and protects you from feeling constantly frustrated. Countless young men and women find themselves in a formidable situation that neither offers a choice nor the hope that something will eventually turn up. Coaching classes provide access to a peer group where everyone is faced with a similar, chronic crisis. Lakhs of students from rural and semi-urban backgrounds spend their youth getting coached indiscriminately for competitive entry into an ever-shrinking opportunity market. Every year, a new army of candidates for coaching is spewed out by rural schools. Many are absorbed into the coaching industry itself, or in its ancillary industry of private tuition.

Rural Alienation

Despite better connectivity by road and phone, villages continue to be alienated from the state's imagination. The former finance minister, P. Chidambaram, once said that migration from rural areas has a positive side to it because the state's services are more accessible in cities. His belief that changes in the rural–urban ratio of population will accelerate development is widely shared. It underpins development planning, especially the project of 'rural development'. In 'Indian Village', a historical study of the Indian village, Manish Thakur has demonstrated how the term 'rural development' represents an essentially colonial view of the village. This view also enjoys political and academic consensus. According to this view, modernity for the village can only mean its merging with the urban landscape. The legitimacy granted to panchayati raj has not diminished the political isolation of the village. The recent protests in Mandsaur and surrounding areas show that higher productivity and relative prosperity have not given the farming community any political clout or relief from uncertainty.

Education could have been a means of integrating the rural into the larger political community symbolised by the nation. This did not happen for several reasons. To begin with, schools in rural areas remained neglected, and attempts to improve them never gained momentum. Policy focus remained on selecting the talented from among rural children, through schemes like the Navodaya Vidyalaya. The larger cohort of rural children suffered the consequences of low budgeting and poor staffing. The message that rural children received and absorbed was that they must change their behaviour and values in order to become good citizens. Education of the rural child has failed to depart from the stereotype which associates modernity with city life. Education has, indeed, exacerbated the rural–urban asymmetry, deepening the alienation of the rural citizen.

Farmers or Peasants?

An instructive aspect of the media coverage of the recent unrest in rural Madhya Pradesh and Maharashtra is the disappearance of the distinction between farmers and peasants. Most people involved in agriculture in India are small-scale peasants. The term 'farmer' refers to the minority with substantial landholdings. Those who died in Mandsaur at the hands of the police were in all probability peasants, not farmers. Among the tens of thousands who have committed suicide out of despair, perhaps most were peasants. Their despair must be read and respected in the larger picture of visionless development. The loans they had failed to repay were minor by urban standards. Their distress reminds us that India has become morally blind in its hasty leap into what it believes to be modern.

12

The Essentialised Village

A version of this article appeared in The Hindu *on 27 May 2015 under the title 'Let us not Essentialize the Village'.*

Several years ago, I witnessed a key moment in a rural primary school in the Allahabad district of Uttar Pradesh. It was a key moment in that it revealed how casual educational planning in India is in the pursuit of long-term social aims. I was sitting in on a lesson for Class V, watching an old, experienced teacher and the children. There were easily at least fifty students. It was a cold morning, and many of them wore neither shoes nor socks. I knew that while the government distributes free uniforms to schoolchildren, shoes are not included. And socks are, in any case, a complicated matter. Somehow, planners have never accepted socks to be a basic need for children. The lesson that morning was a poem. It was a patriotic piece of verse, with plenty of scope for explaining difficult words and their spelling. That is what the teacher was doing when he noticed that someone was standing at the door and holding a piece of paper. The teacher went over to the door, looked at the paper. Then he turned towards the class and said, 'All the SC [Scheduled Caste] children, stand up.' Some ten or twelve children stood up. The teacher told them, 'Go to the office. Your scholarship has come.' They left and the lesson continued.

As far as the teacher was concerned, there was nothing unusual in referring to some of his students as 'SC children'. Identifying children by their caste background was part of a routine necessity. It was official work—that's all. What about the rest of the children? When I put this question to the teacher during the half-day break, he smiled and said, 'They are general.' That did not answer my question, so I repeated it. He said, 'This is a village. Everyone knows everybody's caste here.' And then he added, 'This is not a city where no one worries about caste.'

A recent visit to Allahabad revived the memory of that teacher and what he had said. This time I had some work in the university. On the way from the station to the guest house, my host updated me with the news. He told me that the process of filling up the hundreds of vacant teaching posts had again stopped because the vice chancellor had resigned. Many prestigious departments were functioning with less than a third of their sanctioned staff strength. This was a familiar story—a sort of national dirge. But something else my host said that morning reminded me of my visit to the village school in Allahabad district. He said that the university functions under the pressure of three main lobbies: the Brahmin group, the Thakur group and the Kayastha group. They actively compete for influence over every major decision and, most avidly, over the process of selection for new appointments. After all, their future depends on continuous recruitment and proof of success in keeping up their pressure.

If there is one city in the north where one might expect caste consciousness to have diminished as a result of modernisation, surely it would be Allahabad. There are several historical reasons for this expectation. To begin with, the university located at Allahabad is among the oldest in India, and it was not merely an examining university. Set up in 1887, it had existed earlier as Muir Central College. With special patronage given by the British to several modern institutions in Allahabad, the university progressed rapidly and became, in popular perception, the 'Oxford of the East'. As historian Christopher Bayly, who passed away recently, has pointed out, the town area of Allahabad had a higher proportion of literates in English than any other town west of Calcutta. With the establishment of the Indian Press in 1884, Allahabad became a major centre of publishing and literary activity in Hindi. The Indian Press launched *Saraswati* in 1900, a monthly magazine that became

Hindi's foremost platform for social and literary debates. As the new century progressed, other journals were born, such as Premchand's *Hans* and Mahadevi Verma's *Chaand*. Remarkably different in their concerns and discourses, these and other magazines deepened the reach of modern ideas in every sphere of social life. The university flourished in the middle of a vast amount of dynamic intellectual, literary and political activity.

Resurgence of Caste

The decline of Allahabad University has a wider, systemic context, but the rise of strong caste-based groups inside it is a more specific phenomenon. It demonstrates the resilience of the caste system and its identity-giving role. The popular assumption that urban modernity will weaken the power of caste was apparently based on a narrow view of the many functions it serves. Caste continues to be a major social force governing matrimony, socialisation of children, social status, and, in many cases, occupation. Political measures such as universal franchise and reservation were expected to make caste hierarchy irrelevant. Perhaps that did happen, but only to a limited extent and not in every region. Modern living, travel and communication were also supposed to usher in a social order where the individual could practise and enjoy the freedom of choice in all matters. When we look at the growth and number of caste and sub-caste communities that inhabit the internet, we realise how innocent our great expectations from modernity were.

Caste mobilisation on the internet reminds us of the desperate search for identity that Indians continue to make, tapping every possible resource—from nation and religion to caste and sub-caste. Apparently, virtual localism provides the same kind of solace in a globalised environment that a visit during holidays to one's native village provided to earlier generations. It can also be seen as solace for the physical loss of the village where one's grandparents once used to live or perhaps are still living.

Urban–Rural Polarity

Despite this pervasive and vigorous presence of caste in the globalised world of Indian modernity, the belief that caste consciousness is mainly a rural phenomenon persists. 'Urban' and 'rural' continue to be treated as contrasting categories, not merely in popular parlance but also as terms of reference for public policy. The growth of education seems to have strengthened the view that caste—as a system of values and beliefs—now prevails mainly in villages. This stereotyped perception privileges the urban over the rural, making the former a symbol of progress and the latter a symbol of stagnation. This simplistic division has distorted public policy and distribution of financial outlays. Towns and cities claim a disproportionately larger share of attention and money. They represent the future of the nation. On the other hand, villages are believed to represent the past. Occasionally treated as objects of reverence and concern, they receive mainly subsistence or, at times, compensatory grants from public funds.

Whether it is caste or any other marker of continuity, the ideology of associating it with rural life is highly problematic. This ideology has imparted an ominous ring to the term 'rural development'. As practised today, rural development means pushing the village to copy the town. This vision has no other image of the future to offer to a village except to become urban-like. This kind of mono-modernism is doomed to fail as indeed it already has. The persistence of caste and its resurgence in modernised spaces prove that policies based on rural–urban polarity are mistaken. Such policies are likely to exacerbate the wider crisis that we can witness across towns and villages in various forms, both in the natural and the social environment. It is a false belief that caste-based identities are a rural preserve. It would be equally erroneous to think that gender bias is found mainly in villages. Such ideas are remarkably popular among those responsible for shaping and implementing state policies, such as civil servants and teachers.

If the only future we can see for villages is to turn them into towns, it would be no future worth aspiring for, considering the shape our towns are already in. The late Raymond Williams, a historian of culture, had pointed out that the country and the city are not two rival states of human reality but rather a continuum with many intermediate forms and overlaps. By essentialising the village, we merely display the limitations of our capacity to acknowledge a general crisis that the agenda of modernity faces.

13

Adolescent Voices

A version of this article appeared in The Hindu *on 29 December 2017 under the title 'Listen to These Four Girls: On the Panapakkam Suicides'.*

Panapakkam is a rural town in Tamil Nadu's Vellore district. Last month, it was in the news when four adolescent girls disappeared from their school, leaving their bags behind. Their shoes were later found beside a sizeable well into which they had apparently jumped in order to end their lives. They were students of Class XI. This is precisely the grade level at which a vast number of India's adolescents feel seriously unhappy and resentful. If you consult a typical textbook on adolescent psychology, you will find such emotions to be common. The text will probably dwell on identity, self-worth and petulance. Teachers are taught about these common symptoms, and those who learn them well enough to discuss them correctly get through their B.Ed. exam without much cramming. When they become teachers, they soon realise that passing the B.Ed. exam is a lot easier than dealing with real adolescents—boys or girls. The Panapakkam girls are reported to have been scolded by a teacher for their poor academic performances and told to call their parents. The girls decided to avoid that ordeal and embraced death instead, thereby displaying another familiar characteristic of the adolescent mind, namely, its preference for comradery in taking a decision.

As a nation, our record of dealing with adolescents is rather poor. To be an adolescent means that you don't feel comfortable with all that is going on around you, but older people don't find it easy to deal with you. This is partly because adolescent behaviour is often prickly and petulant. The larger reason, however, is that adolescents live in an ideal world and measure everyone, including parents and teachers, by their utopian standards. This is not merely an emotional response to an imperfect world; it is also proof of their fully developed logical capacity. By defying the adults surrounding them, adolescents develop their own identity as individuals. This is not easy, so they depend on their peers to plan and decide. Their private fantasies are mostly benign and transformative. We can say that adolescent dreams represent a nation's wealth. In India, this wealth is mostly burnt up in preparation for exams.

Ignoring or oppressing adolescents is not uncommon in other countries, but India's case is somewhat extreme. For more than a century, our system of schooling has honed its tools to oppress and defeat the adolescent. The tool used to subdue the rebellious adolescent mind is the Board exam. The term 'Board' has acquired connotations of terror for the young on account of the darkness into which it pushes them before some are let back out into the light of further education. Boards of exam maintain a tight secrecy over how a young student will be marked and declared either 'pass' or 'fail'. Social history is rife with instances of unwarranted failure and the opprobrium of family seniors.

The matriculation exam is part of family lore in every region of India. Fear of failing in it, and thereby closing off all doors to a worthwhile future, figures in many autobiographies written during the colonial period. Exam mania is instilled into the young mind from the start of primary schooling. Popular understanding of education, which is widely shared in political and official circles, equates learning with exam performance. The nationwide industry that specialises in offering help in passing exams and entrance tests makes no distinction between cramming, cheating and learning. The Class X exam continues to 'fail' millions every summer.

If an adolescent successfully survives the Class X exam, his or her ordeal enters a more complicated phase involving the choice of subjects for the higher secondary exam. The Panapakkam girls who chose to end their lives were studying in Class XI. We do not know what subjects they had selected to study in this fateful class. For a vast majority of students moving into Class XI, the choice of elective subjects is made by their parents or senior siblings and teachers. Subjects are seen as tickets to the future. Some are regarded as reliable tickets for a coveted future while others are seen as bogus tickets, carrying the risk of lifelong stagnation. These are, of course, stereotypes, but they persist as currency of practical wisdom in a blind market controlled by Boards. No principal, teacher or parent dares to demand openness from a Board about its procedures. A tight cover of confidentiality is maintained to conceal the abysmal quality of the marking system, question papers and the evaluation process.

In the case of girls, school-related anxieties are compounded by older, entrenched anxieties associated with gendering. Family and kinship fuel the apprehensions that girls internalise from early childhood onwards about their matrimonial future. Educating a daughter is often perceived as an investment towards her marriage. The fear of being viewed as a poor performer at school adds to the stress at home. Teachers usually have scant awareness of their students' state of mind. When they ask students to bring parents to school, they assume this will create additional pressure to encourage harder work. This simplistic logic carries great risk as the Panapakkam incident shows.

The state of education being what it is at present, it is unlikely that the voices drowned in the well at Panapakkam will be heard, but an effort must be made to do so. Boards responsible for the examination industry must realise that that it is no longer useful to install helplines to provide just-in-time advice for a sixteen-year-old in despair. The entire Board exam system and the culture associated with it constitute an endemic problem. Plenty of ideas for reforming the boards and the exam system they govern have been given over the years. Some of these ideas have been put into practise here and there, as isolated steps lacking a wider frame of reference to curricular reform. The National Curriculum Framework (NCF), 2005, insisted on coherence between reforms in curriculum, examinations and teacher training. This perspective continues to pose a challenge to an institutional structure marked by rivalry and turf wars. Those who are in charge of curriculum reforms have little say in exam reforms. Without any exception, the absence of understanding and coordination between the two prevails in states, and the Centre has so far not been able to set an example.

14

Remembering a Baiga Woman

A version of this article appeared in The Hindu *on 29 November 2014 under the title 'Chaiti Bai's Story and Modern India'.*

A sudden death always carries great pedagogical value. The death of Chaiti Bai, a Baiga woman, following a botched tubectomy at a mass sterilisation camp in Chhattisgarh, can improve our perspective on India's history as a modern nation. She was one of the fourteen women who gained momentary national attention after a state doctor had operated on them in an unclean medical camp and they died. The middle of November, when the incident happened, marks the birth anniversary of Nehru and the opening of New Delhi's India International Trade Fair. Both events had special status this year. Chaiti Bai and her death mates give us an opportunity to reflect on the problems India faces in the pursuit of modernity and global status through rapid industrial progress.

An early achievement of this vision is located within a three-hour car ride from the villages where Chaiti Bai and the other young women were killed in a poorly planned surgical exercise. I am referring to Bhilai, where one of the three gigantic steel plants was set up by the new nation state in the 1950s with the help of friendly foreign nations. It made eminent sense to set up a modern steel plant in this economically backward area because a vast deposit of iron ore lies buried under the earth's surface here. The problem is above the surface, and it has two parts: one, a dense forest; and two, a substantial population of tribal people. Chaiti Bai belonged to a small tribe known as the Baiga. Performing a tubectomy on Chaiti Bai was an illegal act because there is a ban on the sterilisation of any Baiga person. This is one of the few civic attainments of this unique tribe. Their numbers are declining, and the Constitution of India protects every Scheduled Tribe from extinction.

Children's Knowledge

In India's tribal world, the Baiga are reputed for their gift of medical knowledge. They inherit and practise an ancient tradition of healing with substances derived from trees and plants. How this knowledge is transferred to the young was the subject of research carried out by Dr Padma Sarangapani in 2003. During her walks with nine-year-old Baiga boys and girls, she found that they could recognise by name and distinguish the medicinal properties of sixty trees. 'They stopped their list,' she writes, 'because of consideration for me because I could no longer keep track.' Dr Sarangapani lamented the indifference shown to this knowledge by school teachers. As expected, they teach the official curriculum. The system is not tuned for showing respect for a child's knowledge, and Baiga children are no exception. They are treated like any group of poor, backward children. The schools they attend aim at routine goals like basic numeracy and literacy.

All the young women who died in Bilaspur were literate enough to sign away their fertility for small sums of money. Their signatures imparted legality to their sterilisation. Literate they were, but not educated enough to know what risks they might run, starting with the risk of contracting infection from a dirty floor. Their exposure to modern schooling had not sufficed to impart the confidence to resist the persuasive pressure of an experienced male doctor determined to meet his personal tubectomy targets for the year. The women who died were poor. One of them is reported to have screamed in pain. The doctor shouted her down and carried on his business. From these women who are now dead we learn that insubstantial and irrelevant education is also inconsequential. India has sophisticated technologies in communication, aviation and warfare, but its schools are crude. Why India's record in elementary education remains so modest needs no commission of enquiry. In a public lecture delivered in the 1980s, Amartya Sen had explained the reason for our educational backwardness by using the proverb, 'as you sow, so you reap'. We never made significant investments in children's education, so we should not expect wonderful results. Underneath this general story of neglect, however, lie the details of an iniquitous system. Between the provisions for an average village school and a Kendriya Vidyalaya, the gap is as vast as the social distance between a small-scale peasant and a civil servant.

Tribes and the State

Children's education has never been a major part of anyone's vision of prosperity and progress. Some may see this as an oxymoron and ask: 'How can progress be achieved without education?' They should ask a more basic question: 'How can progress be achieved without health?' Surely health is more basic than education. Since Independence, both these areas of welfare have been consistently served by rhetoric and neglect. The only major change visible in the recent decades is the state's careful manoeuvres to withdraw without being noticed, enabling commercial interests to take over. Areas designated as 'tribal' are no exception to this general trend. The paradox they represent in the story of development is not radically different from what rural India in general represents. India's aspiration to become a modern nation presented a problem as soon as the drafting of the Constitution began following the end of colonial rule. The problem had to do with defining the civic rights of the tribes. Simply put, the question was to decide the extent of the rights the tribes would have with regard to the forests they inhabited and used freely for their livelihood. The question was not unique to India, nor was the legal solution that India adopted unique.

It was decided that the tribal people could not claim a sovereign right on the forests and the minerals that lay underneath. The state's sovereignty would extend to these resources, and in return, so to say, the state would promise to protect the tribes and treat them as a privileged category in welfare policies and provisions. Had this privileged position of the tribes been translated into action, it would have meant a sophisticated system of education adjusted to tribal cultures, languages and knowledge. It would have meant differentiating among tribes and equipping the system to handle curricular and training details with specificity. As time went by, it became clear that the state was going to remain colonial in its outlook and actions. Tribal areas did receive certain privileges, but they were not sufficient to protect tribal people from the aggressive greed of developers and contractors. Soon enough, the state's resolve and sense of purpose was lost in a jungle of programmes and demands. Stark instances of this process surfaced all over tribal regions. A recent one was the trial inoculation of thousands of girls studying in residential tribal schools in Andhra Pradesh against cervical cancer. Global pharmaceutical interests had succeeded in obtaining the state government's approval. The state assumed that it could act *on behalf of* the girls.

Chhattisgarh's medical disaster shows how helpless tribal people are. When Chhattisgarh was carved out of Madhya Pradesh, and Jharkhand from Bihar, it was assumed that smaller states would focus more efficiently—and sensitively too—on tribal issues. Fourteen years on, one has reasons to doubt the thesis that smaller political and administrative units are necessarily better. On the contrary, the lack of perspective persists. And in the context of tribal issues, it is not merely a question of perspective. State players perceive the tribes through an ideological screen that makes tribal life and culture look like an obstacle to modernisation.

During the recent years, Chhattisgarh has been in the news for a state programme called Salwa Judum that was launched to counter Maoism. Tens of thousands of tribal people have been displaced into camps under this programme, perpetuating the cycle of violence and misery. Political leaders and officers see it as a major attempt to reorganise the balance of forces in Chhattisgarh so as to prepare it for globalisation of the economy. But the region joined the global economy a long time ago when the export of iron ore to Japan from the Bailadila mines in Bastar started. During a lecture delivered nearly thirty years ago, M. N. Buch, a former Chief Secretary of Madhya Pradesh, showed pictures of the landscape around these mines. His dire prediction that mining on this scale would turn the dense forest into a desert seemed reasonable. He was in despair about the impact of the untrammelled exploitation of natural resources on the precarious life of the tribes. The deaths of Chaiti Bai and other tribal women justify Buch's ominous prediction and despair.

REFERENCES

Sarangapani, Padma M. 2003. 'Indigenising Curriculum: Questions posed by Baiga.' *Vidya, Comparative Education* 39(2):199–209. doi: 10.1080/03050060302552.

15

The Temptation to Take a Picture

A version of this article appeared in The Hindu *on 10 February 2017 under the title 'The Temptation to Go Viral'.*

Newspapers recently carried a story about a young man who lay bleeding on the road while onlookers took pictures and filmed videos of him. The incident occurred in Koppal in Karnataka. The bicycle this eighteen-year-old was riding was caught under the rear wheel of a state bus. Though he emerged alive, he was badly injured and crying for help. Apparently, bystanders couldn't figure out how to help him, but they used their mobile phones to take pictures. A video of his suffering soon went viral, as they say, suggesting that it became visual material worth watching. An ambulance eventually arrived and took the young man to a hospital, but the doctors there could not save him. Had he been brought sooner, they said, he might have survived.

An instantaneous gathering of curious onlookers is common in our part of the world. Anything new or unusual spotted on the street makes people stop and stare. When an accident occurs, a traffic jam follows, not always because the vehicles passing by have less space, but mostly because drivers slow down to take a good look at the accident. Cyclists place one foot down on the ground and pedestrians gather. Curiosity alone can't explain this behaviour, for no one seems satisfied with one good look. People keep staring as if they are waiting for something to happen. They realise that the police should turn up in a short while and then something *will* happen, so there *will* be more to see. The scene finds resonance in our mythology and history; it suggests a deep reluctance to take initiative or to get involved. Once a crowd gathers, the lone individual who might be inclined to take initiative also loses the instinct to do so, simply because a crowd—any crowd—discourages individuality. The pressure to behave like everybody else greatly increases when you stand in a mass. So it is natural for people standing in a crowd to simply stare rather than to do something.

The mobile phone's capacity to serve as a handy camera has added a new dimension to this familiar story. If a crowd has accumulated for no particular reason or cause but merely to stare, and the people assembled have a common reluctance to do something or get involved, the camera function of the mobile phone provides a nice outlet for everyone's somewhat confused energy. The idea of taking a picture creates the option of having something to do. It presents an attractive opportunity of sending the picture across to your friends and anyone else interested. The desire to share a picture instantly by placing it on social media is a new kind of behaviour in the history of crowds. Having witnessed it among students during excursions, I think it creates the satisfaction of doing something, apart from in itself being somewhat exciting. A screen picture in colour looks sharp and bright; taking and transmitting it offer the contentment of capturing something one has come across. It channelises and disperses the sense of personal responsibility one might feel as a witness to something awful. The fact that I have sent the picture to others spread across my country, and even across other countries, liberates me from the gnawing thought that I did nothing because I was paralysed or scared. At the very least, it offers some relief from the feeling that I watched someone bleed and just stood there doing nothing. It provides the satisfaction of doing something while maintaining the relief that I am not getting involved in something that might cause serious inconvenience later.

Good Samaritan Law

Karnataka now has a Good Samaritan law that protects the kind-hearted citizen who helps an accident victim from police harassment. The enactment of such a law undoubtedly marks a step towards change in onlooker behaviour as it acknowledges an old source of fear. Apparently, the Good Samaritan law has not sufficed to create the confidence it takes to act in a scene like the one witnessed in Koppal. Apart from confidence, one must also feel like taking initiative. Reluctance to do something is habitually guided by the apprehension that the consequences of involvement can't be predicted or controlled. This feeling runs deeper in district towns where the institutions of the state, such as the police, don't always convey a sense of security to the common citizen who is not a local 'notable'—a term colonial district officers were fond of. Anyone who has faced questioning by the police in a provincial town or village knows what it takes to breathe without fear in the presence of a police officer. Let us imagine that someone who saw the accident in Koppal took the initiative to stop a car and rode in it with the injured youth to a hospital. This would surely leave bloodstains in the car and one of the bystanders would have captured its number plate on the mobile camera. It takes mature sensibility and respect for ordinary people to avoid probing them unnecessarily before declaring them to be good samaritans. Distinguishing good involvement from bad in a scene of crime demands significant levels of training and perspicacity. Long, very long and circuitous questioning by the police has been the norm since colonial days, and during such sessions the person who is not the perpetrator of a crime but merely a helper of the victim is subjected to the same routine ruthlessness that the perpetrator might deserve. If you think your role is over once you have transported the victim to a nearby hospital, you are likely to be proved mistaken.

These are early days in the history of the Good Samaritan law. It will take a long time for people to feel secure under its provisions. Any law that attempts to change people's perception of a state agency demands a parallel change in the behaviour of the agency itself. In this case, it is the police. Reforms in the system of investigation, articulated and recommended decades ago, have been waiting to be implemented. Both the will and the resources required for implementing them are in short supply. It is anybody's guess whether the police in Karnataka understand and accept the Good Samaritan law. If they do, and if, in a few cases, they act according to it, they will have to publicise the names of many good samaritans over the coming years and decades to have a positive impact on the public, on its insecurity and apprehensions.

Mobile Phone as Camera

But what about taking pictures? This behaviour has risen remarkably rapidly over the last two decades. The mobile phone has transformed the meaning of photography. You can now take countless pictures without worrying about exhausting a reel. You are equipped to take pictures all the time and everywhere. No matter where you may take young students on an excursion, as soon as they get there, they start taking pictures. Neither the solemnity of a place nor its rarity makes any difference. Their urge to capture everything in their mobile has turned into a compulsion. The object does not matter; it can be a flower, a poster or a bleeding body. The mobile phone camera serves as a mediator. By creating a distance between the viewer and the object, it neutralises the horror of seeing someone in pain and screaming for help. It thereby also mitigates the guilt one might feel being a mere onlooker.

In their commentary on the Koppal story, readers have berated the loss of sensitivity and values. Quite a few have blamed education. It is difficult to agree with them, although one can understand why education serves so readily as a whipping horse whenever social values are discussed. Administrators and political leaders share with ordinary people a flat notion of education. They don't appreciate what it takes to make education an experience that has the potential to create self-awareness and sensibility. A key resource often underestimated is the teacher. It is fashionable to express frustration with teachers and to recommend technology to control and replace them. As for teachers themselves, they are being pushed hard to cope with the active presence of mobile phones in the classroom. You are supposed to find ways to use students' passion for mobile phones rather than criticise it. And yet, the ideal teacher these days is one who pretends to be unaware that students are busy with their mobile phones, sending and receiving messages and pictures.

16

A Matter of Belief

A version of this essay appeared in Seminar, *issue no. 369, in November 1989. This issue marked the hundredth birth anniversary of Nehru.*

Ganeshganj seems to me an eminently suitable spot in my district where one can sit down under a tree and take stock of Nehru's performance in the shaping of our country's history. The tree I have in mind stands right beside the road to Tikamgarh, the district headquarters, which is less than three kilometres away. You can watch villagers going by on bikes, better-fed youngsters of the town on motorbikes (Rajdoot, or something fancier like a Honda), a Czech tractor with its trolley crowded with men and women labourers, and eventually a packed bus from or to Lalitpur. If you turn around, you can see the tired little structure of a primary school.

It takes some sense of history to accept that this was the site of a heady national-level experiment sixty years ago. A young woman called Prem, who was a community development worker in Ganeshganj, used to teach the village women how to sew and look after babies, and the children how to read and write. She kept the primary school's building in rather nice shape then, but that really was a long time ago.

Between the tree and the school lies the proverbial village pond and a well. The widest lane of Ganeshganj leads from the main road, past the well, into the basti, and then on it winds through some charming Vindhya landscape (fields interspersed by rocky valleys of tough old rivers) to Barighat, about three kilometres away. Here stands, steps away from the confluence of Jaamni and Jamrar, a water-purifying and pumping station which supplies all the water that the ten thousand households of Tikamgarh can use.

Tap water changed life in Tikamgarh during my childhood, especially for women, and that I count as Nehru's best gift of modernisation to Tikamgarh. But although in the vicinity of Barighat, life in Ganeshganj did not change. The pond remains as dirty as ever, and the lane going past the well fills up with nasty mud after a day of decent rain. It is difficult to find any happy traces of community development in Ganeshganj now. The school stares at you like a little boy selling the evening paper at the Safdarjung crossing in New Delhi—defiant of your sensibility, and really very thin-looking.

Ganeshganj has electricity, and the infant mortality rate there must be a shade lower now than it was in Nehru's days, but you cannot tell the difference if you watch the babies that women carry in their arms. Similarly, I am sure literacy must have been recorded one or two percentage points higher in each census succeeding that of 1951. Today (that is, in 1989) it stands at nineteen per cent in Tikamgarh district, and in Ganeshganj it would be roughly on a par with the district's average.

Not far from the tree by the roadside stands the red statue of a shapely horse. Public memory and legend connect this statue with Maharaja Veer Singh's favourite horse who raced against a train and did reasonably well, except that he died in the end. If one is trying to be objective about Nehru's days, one might do well to recall R. K. Narayan's short story 'A Horse and Two Goats'. The scene at Ganeshganj is just the type Narayan depicts in his story. A foreigner wants to buy the statue and assumes that the man grazing his two goats nearby owns it. Thus starts a long and difficult dialogue between two civilisations—one with clearly defined goals and determination, the other with enough ingenuity to let strange things pass.

To my mind, community development at Ganeshganj was a dialogue of this kind. The state, under Nehru's command, spoke its part—goals, expectations and so on. The peasant and the landless labourer spoke what they safely could, given the friendship they noticed between the community development team and the richer, powerful people. I doubt if women or children ever said anything.

In those days, they were just supposed to smile when the Films Division camera was pointing at them.

I could be misconstrued as saying Nehru's vision of India's development was too Westernised, and so it clashed with something innate in our culture. No doubt Nehru's vision of a modernised India was rooted in Western ideas, but this kind of allegation can only excite those people who choose to forget that the struggle for independence was also based on Western ideas. The point I want to make about community development at Ganeshganj is different. The difficulty in the dialogue that community development initiated with the villager lay not in the content of the dialogue, but in the agency.

In all the dreams and plans Nehru had, the state had a key role. It was to act as the mover of a stubborn mass of tradition, as the harbinger of new thoughts and ways of action, and as the repository of all desirable values and ideals. It was supposed to incarnate nationalism, secularism, self-identity and progress. It symbolised the only hope of a society whose kings had lost the right to rule and which had no bourgeoisie with the drive to transform the world. The state thus seemed an appropriate choice for translating new ideas into action. The only problem with this choice was in the nature of the state.

Let me dip into personal history once again before I comment any further on Nehru's reliance on the state and its consequences. My parents were victims of Partition. They could never forgive Nehru for sanctioning a festive ceremony of Independence in the face of the tragic turmoil that was raging in the border states. Why could he not make do with a modest ceremony, my father always asked. The only answer I can find is in my feeling that Nehru did not want the rituals of the state to be marred by the social conditions surrounding him. Not just the ceremony of Independence, but all state festivities and functions were of an order elevated far above society's financial reach, mood and daily woes.

As I grew up, I noticed that ordinary life in my town was spruced up, in fact covered up, whenever a minister or commissioner was on a visit. Public Works Department (PWD) trucks would bring in red, sandy earth, and overnight labourers would spread it neatly on both sides of the main road and in the maidan where the dignitary was to be received. That red earth became in my mind a symbol of the state. Whenever I see that kind of red earth and a shamiana, I am reminded of my childhood conviction that men of the government were not part of us, so they could not be shown the ordinary reality. The other symbol I came to associate with what I saw of Nehru's rule in my childhood was the gamla—a neat device to carry greenery around to welcome the dignitary wherever he went.

The elaborate preparations made for receiving men of the state, the rituals of welcome that are performed when they finally arrive, and the entire exercise of self-deception they agree to go through on such occasions are but residues of colonial rule. Their persistence shows that they are consistent with the nature of the state that the English colonisers constructed and the rulers of Nehru's generation accepted as part of a convenient inheritance.

The construction of the colonial state had begun in the late eighteenth century, and it had rested on the pre-democratic, utilitarian doctrine that eighteenth-century England could provide. According to this doctrine, the class of society that has the maximum stake in the state is that of property owners. The early liberal state was but a reflection of this idea and was meant to serve the owners of property. By the time the liberal state went through its gradual democratic transformation in the England of nineteenth century, the norms of state behaviour, its rules and codes in colonial India were already set.

The liberal state served both the colonial masters and the Indian propertied classes with remarkable ease, especially after the adjustments necessitated by the events of 1857. The social movements that arose in different parts of India around the problem of inequality exercised some pressure on the state on behalf of the downtrodden, but this pressure was not sufficient to reform the state's apparatus, its primary nature and codes. The colonial state was essentially a machinery for the maintenance of law and order. It had little real interest or capacity to acknowledge and improve the dire condition in which India's propertyless masses lived.

Nehru strode ahead to use the state apparatus as if it had had nothing to do with colonisation. He almost did not notice the enormous material and social gap that divided the men placed inside the apparatus of the state, whatever their ranks, from common powerless people. He did complain about bureaucratic functioning and habits, but did not prioritise the task of redefining India's administrative needs and reforming the state apparatus to fulfil these needs. This is where the problems of improving Ganeshganj through community development originated. Ganeshganj became the victim of a big lie. I am willing to call it 'rhetoric' if 'lie' is too unacademic and offensive. An apparatus that had nothing to do with people's welfare and which had specialised all along in the maintenance of order was now suddenly required to uplift the poor peasant, teach women how to look after their babies properly, and design primary education for village children.

Recourse to rhetoric was the only way the bureaucratic apparatus could serve these aims. The representatives of the public that there were, badly needed such rhetoric to legitimise their right to privileges and power. For the poor in Ganeshganj, there was nothing to latch on to in the programme. They knew, as every school lad in our parts knows to this day, that men of the state do not speak the truth—that they only like to see and be told about nice things. I remember the day the governor came to our town. Three freshly killed dacoits were physically laid out for his inspection. My sister had whispered in my ear as I stood in that ceremonious crowd, 'They are not really dacoits, just some ordinary kisans.'

Nehru's India was an exciting, pleasant experience, provided you believed in it. The problem of my generation—born in the years following the midnight of Independence—is precisely that it lost its ability to believe before it had developed the acumen to examine. I really cannot believe, for example, that Nehru wanted Gandhi's basic education plans to succeed. I have examined elsewhere the clash between Nehru and Gandhi's ideas about India's progress. Here it should suffice to say that Gandhi's educational plan was just a shade too outlandish for Nehru's taste. The irony is that though basic education was the only really exciting thing that ever happened in Indian primary schools, Nehru's government could not provide the support and encouragement that basic education needed. It was eaten up by inspectors and directors, and by private interests in the textbook-publishing business. No one in the government seemed particularly sorry about the death of a great idea. Once the idea had been administratively sabotaged, it was put away for good with a 'Didn't we tell you?' kind of laugh.

If Nehru had launched some other scheme to modernise primary education, the death of basic education would not look so tragic after all. But he just talked about primary education, and allowed primary schools to continue as pre-colonial cultural factories of slow, intellectual slaughter. He is on record as having stressed the need to give every possible financial support to primary education, but there is no evidence that shows him worrying about the modernisation of India's primitive primary schools. In his *The Discovery of India* (1946), he mentions the intellectual awakening that a child's peep into the microscope causes. I wonder why he never once asked his economic experts to calculate the cost of equipping every school with a microscope. My hunch is that Khrushchev would have obliged him with such a gift had he presented the problem.

There is always the answer that his life as prime minister was just too preoccupied with graver matters for school conditions to receive his attention. Maybe that is so, if one discounts all those stories S. Gopal records in his biography showing that Nehru always found time for all sorts of little human concerns. My guess is that children's education did not get his attention because he did not have a feel for India's educational problems. The fact that he had escaped the violence that Indian schools commit on little children offers a clue to his failure in making education a national priority.

As one reads about his life as prime minister, one senses that education, especially children's education, would be too humble and routine an area to capture the attention of a great man like him. There was no drama, no debate and no scope for conflict in primary education. There would have been some scope for debate if Nehru had openly criticised the basic education approach, say, as Mulk Raj Anand had done in *On Education* (1947). That kind of debate might have been politically imprudent, but it would have permitted the idea behind basic education to develop. Perhaps an alternative model would have arisen out of such a debate, an alternative devoid of some of the orthodoxies that basic education had accumulated.

No, basic education was permitted to die its own death. An orthodox version of it became the means by which a band of people could be identified. Others were free to criticise it without having the responsibility to develop a substitute. By the beginning of the 1960s, baste schools ('Nai Talim' or Gandhian basic schools) were fading out. The cruel, obsolete pedagogy that had characterised primary schools for centuries (before the advent of colonial rule and during it) was ready to resettle. Only this time, its re-emergence was not to be acknowledged. Rhetoric was to be used in the service of the poorly dressed emperor. New vocabularies and new agencies to disseminate it were ready to take over the job of calling a spade a spacecraft.

Before Nehru died, primary education was heading down the path of rapid decline towards a total neglect of basic aims. But from then onwards, and for a long time to come, no one was going to say that our primary schools were an agency of human resource destruction. The last of the great critics, Gijubhai and Tagore, were dead and forgotten. The 'development decade' of the 1960s gave the intelligentsia a new set of blinkers and the bureaucracy a new set of terms to talk about the country's problems. How could anyone be so blatant as to say that our primary schools were no different from what they had been before the British had come and while they were here? It was far more polite to believe that the NCERT had really started having a modernist impact on teaching and the curriculum.

A copy of the selected statistics from the Fifth All India Educational Survey has just arrived at my desk. I have looked up the enrolment figures for Madhya Pradesh according to which the enrolment in Grade Two is now ninety per cent and in Grade Three about ninety-one per cent in relation to the enrolment in Grade One. These are figures showing the number of names in school registers, not children attending actual classes. The state, I often feel, does not want to hear about children, only their numbers. How should I serve my state if it does not want to hear about reality, when it is the state's prime job to be aware of reality? I have no red sand to spread around. Can the state ever do something about the reality if it does not want to hear about it?

The reality is harsh news, indeed unbelievable news, if we are talking about children's education. Instead of growing or developing, we have regressed in this area, and continue to do so. A mass of miserable instincts and poorly learnt skills are what the human resource reservoir of our youth has become. Nehru would have thought this to be too pessimistic a picture. He taught us to view development as a revolution, and to believe the All India Radio story that development is indeed taking place. Baba Amte opposing the development of the Narmada valley or R. K. Narayan talking in the Rajya Sabha about the daily torture of children in schools would probably have made as little sense to Nehru as they do to his successors in New Delhi today. The continued story of the neglect of primary education got a break when the Right to Education was turned into law, but its dilution started within less than a decade.

17

Citizens and the Bureaucracy

A version of this article appeared in The Hindu *on 5 May 2016 under the title 'The Lone Voice of Pankajakshi Amma'.*

Most images of Kollam depicted the horror of death and injury by fire. The media stories of the tragedy in Kollam describe how a cache of fireworks exploded during the festive season, killing one hundred and injuring close to four hundred. Most images of the tragedy depict the horror of death and injury by fire. Among these images stands out Pankajakshi Amma, who has a house in the vicinity of the site of the explosion. She tried to avert the inferno by writing to the district administration, seeking a ban on competitive fireworks. I am sure the collector and other officials were familiar with this phenomenon, but in our country even the obvious needs to be stated in order to demand the state's intervention. This is how it has been since colonial times. History suggests that after 1857, the civil administration became sensitive about cultural matters and decided to keep aloof from activities rooted in religious custom and rituals.

Disasters are believed to be good learning resources, but it is not easy to know what exactly they teach. Each disaster is somewhat different because it is composed of several local elements that make it specific. Safety is both a public and a private issue. For Pankajakshi Amma, it was a personal concern as she lives close to the temple. Why was the safety of her house not a matter of concern for those who wanted to enjoy the spectacle of competitive fireworks? This is a good question to start a social enquiry into the lesson this calamity can teach us. Perhaps it is too naïve a question to ask in an era and ethos where the right to enjoy takes precedence over concern for safety. When collective enjoyment is at stake—that too as part of a religious ritual—an elderly woman's anxiety over safety seems like a trivial nuisance. Her writing to the district collector was reportedly viewed as downright objectionable behaviour, apparently because it was anti-collective and hence antisocial. Media reports indicate that she was criticised, even threatened, and told to withdraw her complaint. She did not. The district administration acted on it, yet the catastrophe was not prevented. Official enquiry will reveal why, but one gathers the impression that both the organisers and the police underestimated the scale of the hazard. They could not anticipate that something might go so flagrantly wrong as it did.

State and Citizens

What happened at Kollam, and the public commentary it has attracted, suggest the state is responsible for protecting the people from their own instincts. In a number of spheres normally classified as cultural activities, the state is expected to make arrangements for the safe conduct of activities that have obvious potential to turn into disasters. The idea that people might act like citizens who have the capacity to worry about themselves remains alien to our milieu. In the Kollam case, the state was faced with a difficult choice. A concerned citizen appealed to the state to protect her from the noise and risk of competitive fireworks. In response to this appeal, the state administration at the district level issued an order banning the event. But that did not stop the event. It would seem as if the administration knew that its writ does not run in such matters, so it did not go any further than issuing an order to fulfil its duty. Like the organisers, the administration too left the matter to fate, hoping for the best.

Now that the worst has occurred, the administration has a new routine to follow. The post-disaster routine covers rescue and relief, but it also includes disbursal of monetary compensations announced by political leaders. These packages are loudly announced on All India Radio within hours after the final counts of the dead and injured are confirmed. Of course, monetary compensation is important. It deals with victims in two accurate categories and leaves no scope for distinctions within them. The packages are publicised as acts of generosity, to be claimed by the kin of victims by presenting the necessary documents. The state's instrumentalist relationship with the people duly covers all stages of the disaster. It starts with hesitation to interfere and ends with distribution of cheques to rightful claimants.

Kerala is often referred to as a model of development, especially in health and literacy. Kerala achieved a high level of functional literacy almost a century ago. Most of its districts are now believed to be fully literate, a fact that no other state can boast of. The standard explanation for Kerala's achievement in this respect starts with the nineteenth century when literacy found diverse patronage and a competitive spirit in different communities, including caste groups, which led to a speedy spread of literacy among rural folk. This movement was sustained in the early part of the twentieth century by modern forms of political mobilisation, which included the creation of rural libraries. This is an extraordinary history, not to be found anywhere else in India on this scale.

Kerala's Record

Now, a century later, when I heard about competitive fireworks, I felt puzzled. If Kerala had taken full advantage of its progress in literacy and developed a sophisticated system of education, perhaps the competitive spirit in its society might not have shifted from libraries to fireworks. When I visited several rural pockets during the 1990s to assess the National Literacy Mission in Kerala, I found village libraries languishing. Not just rural libraries, Kerala has also permitted its education system to stagnate. Basking in the glory of being India's most literate state, the machinery of governance ignored the challenge of pedagogic modernism. Education remained vulnerable to struggles for cultural dominance. Neither schools nor colleges and universities aspired for the goal of using knowledge for cultural renewal and transformation. The struggle necessary for maintaining the autonomy of knowledge and creativity waned.

Competition over explosive firecrackers is understandably exciting. One can imagine its power to distract and entertain. Spectacles have been part of religious lore and festivals, and with advancement in the technique of using chemicals that cause light and sound, the festive value of firecrackers has greatly increased. This development also suggests greater hunger for sensational stimulation, especially in public spaces. Parallel growth of sensibility and concern for others might have provided a counterbalancing touch. If nothing else, it might have reduced the aggression with which any questioning of sensational, and sometimes cruel, festivities is greeted. Elephants have been part of religious spectacles in Kerala, and cruelty towards them has been debated. They perform an important role in religious festivities in many parts of the country. There have been occasions when elephants cannot take it anymore and run amok, causing stampedes. The legendary cartoonist and children's writer K. Shankar Pillai portrayed one such incident, and transformed it with imagination in his classic story, 'Mahagiri'. In the story, a temple elephant is mercilessly goaded because he refuses to place a wooden pole in his pit. He goes wild, and when everyone has run away, he lowers his trunk into the pit and gently takes out a kitten hiding in it.

It will not be surprising if the official enquiry recommends that lessons on fire safety should be included in textbooks. Every time something awful happens as a result of public or official neglect, a common knee-jerk reaction is to revise the textbooks. Who can deny that textbooks matter? What matters more is how they introduce civic concerns like public safety. Textbooks are often quite stodgy and wooden, so even if they carry some useful lesson, it makes little impact, especially if the impact is expected to last from school days to adulthood. Textbooks avoid focusing on specific stories, so the Kollam tragedy may not make it to a textbook. But if it does, let us hope it will celebrate the lone voice of Pankajakshi Amma. Those who are familiar with small-town India know how bold one must be in order to approach local authorities when neighbours turn a deaf ear. Citizens who ask the police to curb the aggression of loudspeakers are the lonely heroes of our democracy. The state waits for their complaints because it lacks the spontaneous will to engage with its own people. Officers who live in civil lines sleep undisturbed by loud prayers and competitive fireworks. They swing into action when law and order breaks down, then they return to their routines in order to recover from the exhaustion of managing impossible situations.

18

A Pedagogy of Freedom and Peace

A version of this essay appeared in The Making of a Modern Indian Artist-Craftsman: Devi Prasad *(published in 2011) under the title 'A Theory for Education and Peace'.*

To Devi Prasad's life as an artist and as a philosopher-fighter for peace, his experience as a teacher of children lends a special dimension. He taught at Sevagram, and the area of the curriculum he worked in was art. What link can we find between the man who led the War Resisters' International (WRI) and the one who worked with children as an art teacher? Were these merely two phases of his life? Considering how poor a status is accorded to school teachers in our society, and especially to art or craft teachers, I can well imagine that many would regard Devi Prasad's life in London as the Secretary General of WRI as the peak of his public career. Others might perceive him mainly as a great ceramic artist, painter and photographer. Both groups might find it difficult to believe that Devi Prasad developed his theory of peace while working as a children's art teacher. Yet, this is the truth.

As a children's art teacher, Devi Prasad brought together two great approaches to human freedom that Tagore and Gandhi had developed in the context of India's struggle against colonial rule. The two men and their minds were quite different, but they were driven by the same urge which inspired many others during the last two centuries—the urge to examine what meaning of 'freedom' might be applicable to India, given her nature and condition. Both believed that education was a major arena of India's struggle for freedom. The pedagogic cultures they invented look rather different if we study them in terms of the ideas and priorities they were based on. In Devi Prasad's work as a teacher, the two entered into a joint frame; not merely as two pictures fitted into a single frame, but rather as two designs woven into one.

How do we know that this happened and what made it possible? The answer draws our attention to Devi Prasad's rarity as a teacher who wrote about his work as a teacher and theorised about it. His book, *Art, the Basis of Education* (1998), provides us with a dense and reflective account of what he did as a teacher and what it meant. Zakir Husain says in his foreword to this classic, 'I have had the opportunity of seeing his work as well as seeing him work.' Devi Prasad's writing lets us do both these kinds of 'seeing' and, in addition, offers us a theory we sorely need to reconstruct education with the help of art. The theory helps us grasp the thread that ties together Devi Prasad's life as an art teacher, artist and a pacifist. It also offers us a means to understand why education which allows us to stay indifferent to violence and war is no education at all.

Quest for Freedom

Its political significance to other parts of the colonised world apart, India's struggle for freedom had a psychological dimension. The question of why India came under British bondage fascinated several great minds during the nineteenth and twentieth centuries. At least a part of the fascination had to do with the hope that the answer would show an appropriate and adequate meaning of 'freedom' for India. For Gandhi, India was not merely a nation in bondage; it was an idea which had somehow become distorted. India's iconic value as a civilisation inspired Gandhi to differentiate rather sharply between the goal of political freedom and the goal of rule over the 'self' or self-rule. Gandhi perceived himself as an explorer of the inner self, which he called 'truth'. Gandhi denied with grace and finality the status of a superior or victorious model of life to Europe and made it look like an object of sympathy. That was good politics too, but it was primarily a quest for a world rather different from what Europe's ascent had promised to create across the world. Gandhi rejected the European model of prosperity because it was based on war and aggression, both against human beings and against nature.

Gandhi spent his life establishing a different model of life and culture based on non-violence. Education formed an important sphere of this attempt. The emphasis in Gandhi's experiments in education was on self-reliance and ingenuity. Both children and teachers worked with their hands to make life possible, give it purpose and grace, and to realise that people do not need a government to maintain peace. Gandhi developed a new political science which had the capacity to serve both as a historical force against colonialism and as a cultural force against India's sharply stratified social order.

The period during which Gandhi's experiment was unfolding was marked by several other experiments. One with which he interacted closely was Tagore's. The two men and their minds differed in many ways, but they maintained an intense dialogue on vital issues and principles. The dialogue between them and between the institutions they set up inspired many minds to invent new ways to look at the world and to find options for the future. Gandhi's suspicion of the state as an instrument of power, and Tagore's critique of nationalism, form a symmetry which found closely resembling expressions in their pedagogic preferences. Gandhi found in the lives of India's artisans a means to challenge the epistemology of conventional education, both colonial and indigenously Indian. Tagore found in art and poetry an integrating principle capable of healing and regenerating. Historians are now beginning to discover the sources of pain and inspiration in Tagore's life which shaped his particular model of child-centredness. The focus of his institutional endeavour has never been in doubt: it was to use the arts as a means to establish a regime of freedom which might work in tune with nature. In his training at Santiniketan during the years leading to the Second World War, Devi Prasad must have experienced a creative model of life which offered hope for a world preoccupied with the plans and means of self-destruction. The model was based on art, in a wide and generous sense, as a means of fulfilling the self.

Three Principles

The idea of self-discovery through creative endeavour develops into full-blown politics of peace in Devi Prasad's account and analysis of his experience as an art teacher. We can identify three broad principles that underpin this remarkable ideational structure. The *first* is the acceptance of the child's innate urge for freedom to express; the *second* is the fundamental integrity of all art forms and crafts; and the *third* is a predisposition towards peace. Let us briefly examine these three principles one by one

Acceptance of the child's freedom is not merely a recognition of the child's right to freedom, as today's political parlance would suggest, but rather a surrender to nature. Terms like the child's 'agency' might help us to grasp what Devi Prasad wants us to do as teachers. However, the spirit of what we do is as important as what we do or avoid doing. Emphasis on activities is synonymous with progressive pedagogy, so the common tendency to keep children busy in multifarious activities seems justified, especially when the alternative is the conventional practice of making children sit in rows, listen to the teacher's voice, focus on the blackboard and prepare diligently for tests and examinations. Devi Prasad belongs to the school of Maria Montessori, Herbert Read and Sylvia Ashton-Warner, who argued that the child's self has in it a potent expressive force; all we need to do as teachers is to let this force find creative opportunities and media to express itself in a benign and encouraging environment. Art can form a comprehensive basis for growth and education because it has the capacity to accommodate not just the intellect and the emotions, but the soul which forms the uniquely individualised 'secret of childhood', as Montessori called it in her famous book of the same name.

What, then, is art? This question helps us reflect on the second principle of Devi Prasad's educational theory, namely, the fundamental integrity of all art forms and crafts. The division of art into forms and genres, according to status and application, tends to cloud our perception of art as a fundamental principle of life itself. When adults talk about art, their discourse tends to be shaped by the heritage of what has been regarded as art, incorporating views about works of art, especially the ones which have received acclaim. Such parlance leads to rationales for the inclusion of art in the school curriculum, with the goal of identifying and nurturing children who might one day become reputed performers or practitioners. People who think this way apparently ignore the developmental value of art which would apply to all children, not a select few. Then there are those who make a strong distinction between crafts like weaving, pottery, carpentry and so on, and 'arts' as they stand defined in the literate discourses of visual arts, music, dance and theatre. This division has its roots in the class division of society, between 'folk' and 'bourgeois'. Be that as it may, all such divisions hinder us from noticing the meaning that art as creative expression might have in the child's life. Devi Prasad draws upon Franz Cižek's term, 'child art', and his own training under Nandalal Bose, to help us ponder his own experience as an art teacher. His various narratives convey his holistic or inclusive vision of art, which transcends genre, media and social categories like 'artist' and 'artisan'. The vision persuades us to see aesthetics as a pervasive regime of mental nourishment. It offers a sense of proportion and balance, the sensibility of rhythm and tone, and above all, a craving for symmetry. These are the elements of peace which are encapsulated by the third principle of Devi Prasad's educational theory.

Education today is so fundamentally linked to war—both its justification and preparation—that any principle which emphasises the relationship between education and peace is likely to be trivialised or perceived as a nice idea not to be taken to heart. Universality of the human predicament in our times is often forgotten when we choose to feel insecure within a nationalist framework. Both Gandhi and Tagore derided such a framework and underlined the civilisational crisis that the whole of humanity was facing. But then, the moment we refer to peace as a universal need, we invite the criticism that we are ignoring the risks our own country faces and the urgency of socialising children into imagined frames in which they see themselves as being ready to sacrifice their lives for the nation in a violent conflict. The political appeal of such imagined frames cuts across national boundaries and unites the so-called developed countries like the US and Israel with the so-called developing nations like India and Pakistan. Concern for national security and the desire to attain it by stockpiling the latest weapons are but symptomatic of the crisis which reproduces itself in the heart's hollow, and is fed into robust permanence by chronic inequality and injustice. This diagnosis must make it clear that there is no immediate or simple solution to the problem of war. In his position as the Secretary General of WRI, Devi Prasad assiduously mobilised people in diverse national settings to pursue an anti-war agenda in the larger framework of a non-violent lifestyle. What we learn from Devi Prasad's work as an art teacher, and the theory derived from it, is how the true beginnings of a peaceful world order can be made. The experience of aesthetic discipline in childhood has the potential to create a predisposition towards peace or an aversion to war. It is easy to be cynical or critical towards such a view on the grounds that its promised outcome is much too distant. That it undoubtedly is. In its true sense, education requires distant time horizons. Only instrumentalist goals can be realised quickly. Today we are encircled by precisely such goals and our preoccupation with them is deepening the crisis that endemic violence and war signify. Now is the right time to mindfully listen to Devi Prasad's advice. Apart from fundamental sanity, it offers a sense of dignity and a historic role to the teacher of the young.